MW00882315

RESCUE YOUR BUSINESS

*The Business Strategies of a Firefighter
Turned 7 Figure Entrepreneur*

BY

KEVIN TACHER

**Founder & CEO, Independence Title
Fort Lauderdale, Florida**

IF SOMEONE TELLS YOU THAT YOU CAN'T, REMEMBER YOU CAN!

Copyright © 2019 Kevin Tacher.

All rights reserved. No part of this publication may be reproduced, distributed, or transmitted in any form or by any means, including photocopying, recording, or other electronic or mechanical methods, without the prior written permission of the author, except in the case of brief quotations embodied in critical reviews and certain other non-commercial uses permitted by copyright law.

Ordering Information: Quantity sales. Special discounts are available on quantity purchases by corporations, associations, and others. Orders by U.S. trade bookstores and wholesalers.

Please Contact:

Independence Title, Inc.

Phone: 954-335-9305

Email: Media@TitleRate.com

DREAMSTARTERS

www.DreamStartersPublishing.com

Table of Contents

About the Author.. 9

Dedications... 11

Special Dedication 12

Foreword by Frank McKinney 13

Introduction.. 15

Industry Networking 19

Importance of Becoming a Philanthropist.................... 29

Getting a Mentor... 37

Don't be Afraid to Share Your Knowledge.................... 45

Proper Planning for a Stormy Day 51

Road to Financial Freedom.. 59

Set Yourself Apart from Your Competition 65

Become a Master at What You Do.................................. 73

Ask for Testimonials 83

Having a Successful Business Plan 93

What to do when Running Out of Fuel 105

Building a Real Estate Dream Team 111

Leverage Social Media and Brand Recognition 117

How to Get Started..127

Having a Support System (Family)..............................135

Final Assignment...143

About the Author

Kevin Tacher – also known as "The Title King" – is the Founder and Chief Executive Officer of Independence Title Inc., a Fort Lauderdale, Florida based title insurance company. Kevin is an amazon.com best-selling author and national real estate speaker. Featured on NBC as well as in person, Kevin has shared the stage with some of the country's best real estate and motivational speakers.

As a trailblazer in the industry, Kevin founded the nationally recognized website TitleRate.com which is the leading source for title insurance rates, real estate mobile applications and up-to-date real estate information. He values community relationships and is involved with several non-profit organizations across the country. Among his various philanthropic contributions, Kevin and his wife Alana have donated towards reducing the struggles of individuals and families in poverty, helping abused and neglected children, supporting our valued military families, granting wishes case by case, and assisting with disaster relief locally as well as abroad.

Prior to moving to Florida in 2001, Kevin grew up on Long Island, NY where he was a firefighter and Fire Safety Director for the Crowne Plaza Hotel in New York City. He moved to Florida only twenty days before September 11th, 2001 narrowly missing that tragic event. He is grateful for the go in together, get out together beliefs it instilled in him, leaving no one behind.

Professionally, Kevin has worked and held licenses as a mortgage consultant, real estate broker, home insurance agent and title insurance agent. Armed with extensive knowledge and experience in the real estate industry, Kevin opened Independence Title Inc. in

Fort Lauderdale. His previous experience enables him to provide a complete range of knowledge for homeowners and real estate professionals throughout the State of Florida.

Kevin loves traveling, scuba diving, fishing and spending time with friends and family. He enjoys South Florida living with his wife Alana, his daughter Lindsay, his son Jaxon and baby cat Bandito.

To learn more about Kevin Tacher, "The Title King," and how you can receive a full copy of his other books, please visit: TitleRate.com or call 954-335-9305

Dedications

To my incredible children Lindsay & Jaxon … your growth provides a constant source of joy and pride. I thank you for always making me smile and for understanding when I need to work instead of play. I hope that one day you can read this book and understand why I spent so much time working. May your lives continue to be filled with joyous memories. Remember this one thing, todays sacrifice, builds for a greater tomorrow. I hope you read this book one day and too build a life of greatness in whatever you both put your minds to.

To my amazing wife Alana … you have always been so supportive since the first day I met you back in 2010 and have continued to support me through every journey good or bad. Without your encouragement, emotional support and great advice, none of this would have been a success. Thank you and I am proud to share its success with you for many years to come. You really complete my circle of life! You're a great Smom to Lindsay, mother to Jaxon and an even more amazing wife. We truly can accomplish more together than we can do alone.

To my parents Robert and Mary Ann … you've supported me throughout my career and it's greatly appreciated. You have given me a path of great success. As a child, you always gave me the guidance and support I needed in order to get through the rough times and always celebrated the good times. I look forward to being able to share this book with you when it comes out and hopefully you will know your past has shaped me to be an even better person today.

To my grandparents Aron and Trudy… you've laid out a path of true financial success for me to shadow and it's greatly treasured. I've always enjoyed watching your lives expand with greatness. Grandpa, although you are no longer with us, I know you are watching over us and this book certainly has business strategies that I know you instilled in your professional career.

To my mentors and great friends Cyndi, Lex, David and Jim… thank you for your mentorship over the past 15 years. Your commitment to today's success has set me on the path for a greater tomorrow. If it wasn't for you all, I wouldn't be where I am today both personally and professionally. Your support and encouragement are exceptional, and I'm honored to be a part of your world-class team of real estate professionals.

To my entire staff at Independence Title … your dedication and commitment to our mission are greatly appreciated and I thank you for being part of our amazing team of title professionals.

Special Dedication

I would like to make a special dedication to my mother-in-law Eileen Burrell and father-in-law Ken Burrell. Your kindness and devotion to your family will never be forgotten. I will always remember how you displayed my last book so proudly in your office. I know you are both following our journey and always looking over us. You are greatly missed but will never be forgotten.

Foreword by Frank McKinney

You want the kind of person who is trained and willing to run into a blazing, five-alarm fire to rescue you, your family and your business. Would you seize the opportunity to have that person BEFORE the burning building ever caught fire?

If you want to prevent getting caught in the flames or if you are in need of a lifeline for your business, Kevin Tacher and his book *Rescue Your Business* are the absolute perfect fit. Firefighters leave no one behind, and Kevin, a former firefighter turned seven-figure entrepreneur, is your oxygen, your ladder, and your life saver!

In 2010, as the foreclosure crisis was in full swing, I was the keynote speaker at the Florida Foreclosure Convention in Fort Lauderdale, Florida. There, I met a young entrepreneur who, despite the imploding economy, was able to fund the construction of a new concrete home for a family of eight in Haiti through my Caring House Project Foundation (www.chpf.org). Within hours of talking with Kevin, he was already thinking of ways he can fund his second home to help those who have nothing and live in the poorest country in world. To date he has now built four homes, talk about rescuing!

To Kevin, success means you can have everything in life you want, if you will just help other people get what they want. He's helped so many in Haiti as well as right here in the United States, and that my friends, is why you need to read *Rescue Your Business*.

The firefighter connection... In *Rescue Your Business*, Kevin talks about the time he was saved while being trapped inside a house engulfed in flames. What saved his life? Another firefighter, who didn't think twice about it, because he also believed in going in together and more importantly getting out together.

Imagine being inside a room of business people, and you have nowhere to turn. You're scared to talk to anyone because of the fear of rejection. In **Rescue Your Business** Kevin shares how to apply the skills he learned as a firefighter and simply implementing them into networking and building relationships early on in business.

Kevin believes this will prove to be the definitive difference between success and failure. If you fail to build relationships, you will fail to succeed.

"I won't leave you behind…" Kevin writes, "In business, to be able to surpass and be one step ahead of other people, one has to make them into allies...." Kevin continues, "…always placing other people's interest first, will provide long-term success for any business."

Any successful business thrives on competition. Competition is where we learn new skills to grow and be better business owners. If you always live in fear, your business will burn to the ground and it might be too late, even for Kevin, that's why you need to read **Rescue Your Business** NOW!

Over the years, I've mentored and worked with some of the biggest entrepreneurs in the world and rarely have I met someone with even half of the drive and ambition as Kevin. That's why this guy walks his talk, and why **Rescue Your Business** is a must have!
Learn Kevin's strategies today, BEFORE the fire, because believe me it will come and when it does with this book, you'll have all the tools to **Rescue Your Business**!

– **Frank McKinney,** 6x Best-Selling Author, Frank-McKinney.com

Introduction

During my freshman year of high school, at George W. Hewlett High School on Long Island, NY, I was lucky enough to meet Jim Hennessy. Jim was a teacher like no other. He stood by your side to make sure you would never fail. Failure wasn't an option for Jim. I disliked high school very much, I was getting frustrated day after day and lost my mindset and focus. I had dreamed of graduating high school and going on to building a successful career. I knew I only had four years before graduation, and that my window of opportunity was brief, to say the least.

Jim gave me a pep-talk, "It's ok, everybody graduates high school. After you graduate, you'll be able to do anything you put your mind to." Jim was right, he stood by my side until I got the call that I passed my final exam and was cleared to finish my 4 years in high school. I'll never forget where I was when I got this call. It meant school was over and it's time for me to shine.

Remember this, your teacher gets paid to make sure their students succeed. To most teachers, failure is not an option. In order to be passionate about your future and direction in life, you need to have a vision. Some business owners have the understanding, and some have the passion, but you must have both to be successful in business.

So, I finally went on to working in the real world. It wasn't as much fun when you had to provide for yourself and most importantly your family. I went from job to job making other people's businesses more successful then when I got there. All of this while I was a volunteer fire fighter in Woodmere, NY. This was my calling. I went from a junior fire fighter, to a probationary fire fighter, to a real fire fighter where I went running into a fire and had the opportunity to save a life and didn't even get a pay check. Then a few years later I moved up the ranks and completed my time in the department as a Captain. Being a Captain in this amazing organization meant I was able to lead my fellow fire fighters into the burning blaze, while having the responsibility to make sure everyone returned home safe.

In 2001 only 20 days before September 11th, I moved to Florida. I was finally in a position in business where I made the decisions. I decided what I did in business to be a success or a failure, as I was in my first few years in business. Were there challenges? Absolutely, and in this book we will cover many things I learned along the way to **Rescue My Business** making me into the 7-figure entrepreneur I am today.

Rescue Your Business was written as the result of over fifteen years of thought, research, and experience in the South Florida Real Estate market. I'll cover my successes along with my failures. I've been in the real estate industry for many years and have seen a wide array of transactions go smoothly. I've also seen my fair share of transactions that didn't go as well. All in all, I've closed over seven thousand five hundred transactions in my career as a Florida licensed title insurance agent, and I like to think that I've seen just about everything when it comes to buying and selling real estate in South Florida. What I specialize most in, is caring that my clients go in the deal together and leave the deal together making sure everyone gets out unharmed. I want to make sure in each transaction all parties leave the deal better off than when they started.

Amongst the many real estate professionals that are successful, there are even more that are not. In my years of experience, I've seen my fair share of these real estate professionals go out of business.

When it comes to buying and selling real estate, people want to know that they are dealing with honest people. My company **Independence Title Inc.** was founded many years ago with a mission to be the most efficient title company in the industry. It's been my ongoing objective to surpass the standards of service previously offered within the title company industry. We consistently accomplish this by establishing strong relationships with proven strategic alliances, offering competitive pricing, and delivering a satisfying experience, by both anticipating the needs and exceeding the expectations of our clients.

We've also developed the nationally recognized website *TitleRate.com* to help expand learning opportunities for individuals interested in real estate. Our principle is clear and simple: Clients interested in real estate should be equipped with all the tools, strategies, and education necessary to help them achieve great success in their careers, while keeping their property title well protected.

I wrote this book with that same mission in mind: to give the readers tips, suggestions, and educational nuggets that will make a difference in the way they either close their next real estate transaction or run their real estate business.

If you remember one thing from reading *Rescue Your Business*, remember what Frank McKinney stated in his forward "You want the kind of person who is trained and willing to run into a blazing, five-alarm fire to rescue you, your family and your business."

Chapter 1

Industry Networking

As a former firefighter, in addition to my career in the real estate, mortgage and title insurance business, I learned about teamwork and having each other's back. In business and in life, we are in this together, and we don't leave anybody behind. This was made very clear to me back in my firefighter days.

In a house fire, a friend and fellow firefighter, Ray Grawin, saved my life. I had gotten literally caught in a tricky spot and couldn't move. He stayed with me until we could both get out. Even during a flash-over, which is where the room ignites in flames, Ray stayed with me. He was able to unhook me from where I was stuck, and dragged me down the stairs and away from danger. So, when I say he saved my life, I'm not exaggerating.

It was a two-story house. As soon as you came in the door, to the right was the living room and to the left was the kitchen. I was holding the hose, pointing it toward the blaze. Ray kept yelling to me, "It's going to blow, be careful - it's too hot - make sure your neck is covered." It got so hot, we knew we were going to have to retreat, and I'll never forget running down the steps, backing down while still holding the hose, my gear got caught on a wrought iron stair banister. It was almost as if I was welded to that banister. Ray stood by and helped me get untangled. I was scared out of my mind; I was thinking, "Oh my God, I'm going to die. I can't get out of here." The fear paralyzed me, and if I didn't have Ray there, I know I wouldn't have managed to get myself free.

That might seem like a dramatic way to introduce this chapter on the importance of networking and building relationships, but I think it really does illustrate the point. This book and much of my work aren't to benefit me; it's to connect with you and help the business professional, specifically those in the real estate business, to get better, to survive and thrive in this complicated world of real estate.

Maybe I can introduce you to concepts that you wouldn't normally think of. Maybe working with others and networking with colleagues, can help you see things in a different way. How can we help empower each other to not only close one deal, but close ten deals? To truly succeed in this business, and in any business, the importance of building mutually beneficial relationships cannot be understated.

In my own business, after 15 years of doing this type of work, we've built a seven-figure fortress. This was done because of the relationships that we have fostered within the organization, with our clients, vendors, and colleagues. All of these factors work together to build a strong business that can withstand just about any downturn, including economic forces outside of our control. This emphasis on relationships and networking is the focus of this chapter.

This book is specifically written for those of you in the business of buying and selling real estate, as well as investors, real estate brokers, mortgage lenders, and anyone else who is building their career in the real estate field. The relationships you build with your clients, whether they are business-to-business clients or consumer clients, are all critical to your success.

Industry networking involves attending numerous events, talking with and meeting colleagues in your field, and in related fields. These relationships that you build within your business, will help you build the business itself. It's so important to remember that whenever you go into a networking event, that you have to actually network. You need to network with people, constantly, to build a level of trust.

For this to happen, other people in your industry need to know and like you. This needs to happen before they can trust you. Many mentors in my career, along the way have all shared the same philosophy with me. In order for someone to trust you enough to send business your way, which is the key to building a referral-based seven figure business, they have to know and like you first. They can't trust you unless they know, and like you.

This isn't just about doing business with you once, or twice. It's about building the relationships where your colleagues will want to do business with you again, and again, and again. For example, at Independence Title, we just celebrated our 15th anniversary, and many of our clients we have had throughout that history.

One of the lessons that I learned many years ago, when I first got into the real estate business, from a mortgage broker who later became a partner in the title company, was watching him close deal after deal after deal; 3-5 loans a month, just through his own efforts. Now, I was new to Florida and didn't know anyone, so I was really watching him succeed in this business and trying to figure out where his success came from. It became obvious to me that his repeat business, and a high volume of business, all came from referrals.

I asked him one day, "So, what happens when referrals run out?"

He laughed, and replied, "I don't know. Referrals have never run out for me!"

That was an important lesson for me, and when the real estate market basically crashed in 2008, this lesson became even more critical. We watched as numerous mortgage brokerages went from 5-10 loans a month, to 3-5, down to 1-2 each month, to out-of-business. With our emphasis on relationships and referrals, we did the complete opposite.

One of my referral partners, Peter Davidson with ADT Security, said to me "Hey, come to this networking event called

BNI," Business Network International. At that time, I didn't know anything about networking. I didn't know even where to start. I basically sat in my cubicle and closed loans, helped people find houses to invest in, and waited for business to come to me. On top of that, I was deathly afraid of public speaking. But I said to Peter, "Ok, sounds good," since they had an opening for a title company.

The meeting was to start at 7 a.m., so I got there early like I usually do. I was pacing up and down outside of a local country club lobby in Pompano Beach. Up and down, up and down, nervously in the driveway of the country club. I was so nervous to even walk in because there were forty people in the meeting room. I froze.

Paul Efron, who deals with a lot of addiction clients through a rehab facility, walked up to me, introduced himself, grabbed me by my shoulder, and literally pulled me into the meeting room. He introduced me to everyone in the room. I was so nervous; here I was confronting one of my greatest fears, even to this day, of meeting new people and public speaking.

But, I learned a very critical lesson that day…

Referrals don't just come in. You can't sit in your cubicle, office, or place of business and wait for people to knock on your door, looking for you. You have to build the foundation and make sure that people will send business your way. In fact, when I completed the application for membership in that BNI group, with my mortgage, real estate, and title company licenses, the other mortgage broker and real estate broker didn't want me to enter the group because they thought I might steal their clients.

Now, I'm probably about the most ethical person in the industry, and I had absolutely no intention of stealing clients. But these people didn't know me, so they couldn't like me, and they certainly didn't trust me. So, during the interview process to join the group, I just did my best to let them know who I was, and how I had no intention of stealing any business from them. I knew that we could work together and refer clients to each other throughout the year.

Over the course of several years in that BNI group, I became the biggest generator of referrals for the entire group. During those six years, I generated over 15% of the revenue of the group through my networking efforts. I knew that if I came to the group, and gave it all, giving out referral after referral, I would in turn, receive referral after referral.

The members of that group quickly got to know me, and I made sure to build meaningful relationships within the group. From there, the other members grew to like me, and then, to trust me. About two years into my membership in the group, someone asked how I was doing in the group. At that time, I was getting a referral or two from other group members, but I was thinking that I was putting more effort into giving referrals than I was getting back in referrals. It felt like a low return on my investment of time and money.

Thinking about it, I remembered with the idea of the "Whale." How do you find the referral source, as opposed to the referral itself? While thinking about this, I knew I had to look bigger than I had. Someone finally introduced me to a real estate broker, who later told me, she saw me shaking in the corner, hiding behind my vendor table at an event. Still nervous, even after two years in the BNI group.

But, she eventually offered me to be her exclusive title company with her real estate firm; one with over 800 agents, and one of the largest in South Florida. This relationship was built from, getting to know me, like me and trust me. I add value to her organization just by being there and being a top affiliate who has taken great care of her agents. We are helping each others' businesses grow.

This is just one example of why industry networking is really important for you to understand. Step out from behind your table and move beyond passing around your business cards, and simply meeting people. It's more about going into the event with say, three of your business cards and meeting three people. Maybe one of those three will turn into a referral partner for you.

So many people go to these events, and they're looking for the referral itself. But, that's self-limiting; there's so much more than the referral. Find the referral source. Meet that person. Get to know them, be likable, and trustworthy. The referrals will follow. Building that type of relationship will turn into an endless stream of referrals for you.

Some tips to connect with other people and build those relationships, is to primarily stay in contact with people. It's not about taking people out for a golf game, or drinks, but staying in meaningful contact. Get to know them as a person. Understand who they are, who they care about, and what it is that they need.

As I advise my staff, get a touch-point with them, at least once a week. What I mean by that is touching base, weekly; it can be a quick phone call, a text, an email or meeting. This could be sending them a news article that might be of interest to them, or sending a link to an industry update. If you can then also have face-to-face contact with them once a month, even better. This will help keep you on the top of their mind.

This type of weekly connection needs to be something that is valuable for THEM. So many people think of what's in it for "me." Shift that focus, and look at what you can do to help your colleague, and build that trust in your relationship with them. Shift the focus from "me," to "you." Find things that will help your businesses grow, together. Develop that endless stream of referrals so everyone benefits.

This, works out to help me greatly, for example, if I can help a Realtor find an endless stream of customers and referrals, I, in turn, get an endless stream of closing referrals. It's really that simple. I help "you," and "you" in turn will want help me.

Going to a networking event, handing out a bunch of business cards, collecting business cards from others, adding them to some sort of email list, and then waiting for them to call you....it just doesn't work that way. You have to personalize and offer meaningful information, get to know that person, listen and learn, and then develop the mutual trust that is needed to create a referral machine.

Social media can help with this; in our office, we use Facebook and Instagram; we provide video newsletters, educating our clients on things that people ask us, and professionally produce them. Most are about 3-5 minutes long and cover a variety of topics in the industry. Right now, we have about 125 of them. I don't include a blurb that tells our audience, "Hey, call me if you need a closing." No, this is just a value added product and service that we provide, to keep our company in their minds when it's time to refer a closing. I don't ask for the business directly. I ask for the relationship, that turns into the referral, that turns into continued business. We provide our clients with great service, at a good price, and we stand behind that product. We fix mistakes and we honor and respect our clients' needs. That's what creates a seven-figure business model.

RESCUE YOUR BUSINESS ASSIGNMENT

Attend a networking event, and follow-up with three contacts, on a weekly basis. Send an email, phone call, text or other communication. Remember, do NOT ask for business. Simply build the relationships.

After 3 months, check-in here, and review your progress with each contact.

1.

2.

3.

What kinds of referrals can you provide for industry-related colleagues?

_____

_____

_____

"Lead, Follow or Get Out of the Way... In business, opportunities can either be stepping stones or stumbling blocks. When building your referral network in challenging economic times it's a matter of how you view them and which path you decide to journey down. If the path you take inspires others to go further and reach higher, then you are a leader."

Kevin Tacher

Chapter 2

Importance of Becoming a Philanthropist

This is one of the most fulfilling lessons that I think ties into the notion of having a seven-figure business. I always tell people that when I talk about this concept, they often reply, "Well, charity is all about giving." And, as much as I agree with that, I think it's more. Honestly, it's not a totally selfless act.

When you talk about being a philanthropist, giving to charity and volunteering, there is a selfishness to it, because it's giving you a feeling. You feel good about yourself when you help out others, when you give to charity and when you are giving back to your community.

At a recent event I spoke at, I talked about volunteering for Habitat for Humanity. An attendee told me that when he volunteers, he tries to hit other volunteers up for business. "That's not what we're trying to do here," I said. I'm not looking for business by volunteering or donating services or funds; that's not what I mean by philanthropy being somewhat selfish. It's giving me the feeling in my heart that makes me feel good about myself and my actions.

My wife and I have our own charity that we love to work on and support, granting wishes for people who have a terminal illness.

We are both passionate about this work; there are so many family members that are affected by the person who is sick, so we like to do things for the entire family including the caretakers.

We've sent families to experience things together like a visit to Disney World, boating, or other adventures. We started this about three years ago, and it's been incredibly rewarding. Once, we took 84 children to the Miami Sea Aquarium; these are kids, who live two miles from the beach but never get to go, some had never been. That felt great. You can't even imagine the faces on these kids when they walked into the aquarium and saw real dolphins swimming by them.

One Christmas, we were asked to sponsor five or ten children for gifts and food. My wife looked at me and said, "No, five or ten isn't enough...let's take fifteen." But, then my wife added, "Well, how many children do you have in the program?" The answer was twenty-six. "Well, we'll sponsor them all," she said. Our entire house was filled with tables of gifts, and we purchased everything they wanted. It wasn't just about the presents they wanted, so many of these kids were asking for gift certificates so that they could take their foster parent to dinner or on a family outing. My wife made it even more personalized by giving them each a custom pillowcase with their name on it, so they could take it to whatever home they were placed in.

We started the charity because we had been giving a lot to local charities, but weren't quite feeling the individual connection with the cause as we would have liked. It wasn't that the local charities weren't appreciating the donation, it's just that we weren't in the thick of it and didn't really get to see any direct result of our donation. It seemed so generic and disassociated with the work at hand.

Our charity isn't organized as a 501(c)(3), or as a tax deduction. We just write the check. We give those funds away so that these families can have the experience of a lifetime, one they will never forget. We want them to have the experience; we want them to be able to momentarily forget about what's going on in their life. Even if it is just for a day, a week or maybe the weekend.

Not that long ago, we met a little girl who had cancer. She was eight or nine years old, and her dream was to go to Disney World. We happily sent her entire family to spend some amazing time, including a retreat at the Gaylord Palms, a resort in nearby Kissimmee. We also reached out to individuals in the community to help give this family the best possible experience they could ever have. They had a VIP experience at the hotel, tickets to Disney World, her name was on the "Welcome" board when they entered the hotel; everyone in the hotel knew who she was, and why she was there, and they made her a SUPER VIP for the weekend. I get chills thinking about it, still to this day.

So, there's the selfishness. I do it, because it makes me feel good. The fact that after a bit of time, I still get chills thinking about that little girl, her family, and the experience we were able to provide, shows the benefit, that I personally receive. But, that's ok. Most people give to charity because it makes them feel good, and if we're being honest with ourselves, there's nothing wrong with that.

In some ways, I think there is a bit of self-fulfilling prophecy when you set yourself up to be a philanthropist. In your mind, when you create ideas in your head, and then what you think about, often comes to fruition. So, when I'm giving to charity, whether it's in my industry or not, for me it's making me feel like a better person.

People do business with people they know, like and trust, so if they know I'm a nice guy, and know that I love giving back to the community, I might gain their business. People who are also giving-minded might see that I'm giving back to the community, so funds from a closing will go back into the local community, they can often feel good about themselves, as well.

This is a classic win-win. It points to the person that you are. You may not have the money to donate to charity. It's ok - it's not about the money. It's about the experience and the feeling; if you don't have excess funds, go volunteer in the community. Give back that way. It doesn't have to be anything big. I tell my dad all the time to go to the local senior center and play cards with someone. Make them feel good, and in return, you'll feel good and you'll be a better person.

This is important for all of us to do, in order to be a better person. I'm not saying you're going to make money by donating to charity, or volunteering in the community. But, by doing so, you're going to be a better person, and you'll put positive energy out into the community. People will see you and know that you're a good person, and they'll just naturally think of you when it comes time to partner with you and your business.

"Giver's Gain," is a philosophy I learned from my time in BNI. Give without any expectation to receive. One of my mentors, Bob Burg, says, "You want to give more in value than you receive in payment." If you give more in value, it will turn around and you will receive ten-fold. But, just don't expect it. Don't give because you're expecting it to come back. Don't say, "I'm going to this charity event so that I can network and make money back," Say to yourself, "I'm going to give, and by giving, and doing the right thing for our community, I'm going to receive good things in life."

It's so important to get involved in charity at some level. It doesn't have to be money. It could be time. It just needs to be something that will make you feel good at the end of the day, knowing you helped someone. It's that simple.

All of my firefighting career was as a volunteer fireman; my first firefighting position was right after high school. My mother has said that as a child, I always wanted to help people. My father is the kind of guy that would give you the shirt off his back if you needed it. I was always taught to do the right thing and to give people something that they didn't have. Being a firefighter for all those years, it was always about helping others when they couldn't help themselves. Most of the time, I was volunteering while I was still working full-time; it was that important to me.

This doesn't make me special. Many people have this in them; some people choose careers that demonstrate this; teachers, military personnel, firefighters, policemen and women. They have a unique role that they're running into difficulty when everyone else is running out.

My daughter attends a school where there was a school shooting. For me, what was amazing was to watch all of the people who were running into that building when the shooting was still active. There were some who didn't, and that's been a controversy. But, there were so many who didn't even think about it - they ran into the danger. There were teachers and students who jumped in front of other students, when others were running away.

This may be an extreme example, but it goes back to my point. Whenever you're able, you have to give to others and help others who can't help themselves.

Twenty days before 9/11, I relocated to Florida; I had been a volunteer firefighter on Long Island, NY, and members of my crew were part of the mayhem of those days and the months of search and rescue, and then recovering bodies. I have a friend who died from after effects of that tragic day.

If I had been in New York that day, I know.. I would have run out of the hotel where I was working and gotten myself into downtown Manhattan to see how I could help. I would have joined my crew from Long Island and been there for the aftermath, to help out my community. Again, this doesn't make me special, it's just how I'm wired.

I can't emphasize enough how important it is to give back. If you're not naturally wired to help out in this way, develop it, and I you will feel the true satisfaction there is in giving back and helping those who need it the most.

RESCUE YOUR BUSINESS ASSIGNMENT

Make a list of organizations that you think are doing great work in your community. How can you help? With money? Volunteering? Become a board member? Sponsoring an event?

_____

_____

_____

_____

_____

Which two or three charities are you willing to give time and/or money to?

_____

_____

_____

_____

_____

_____

"Each one of us has been blessed with the ability to succeed. Once we realize these blessings aren't meant for our sole benefit, but must be used in order to assist those less fortunate, the 'more' we pray for may be granted."

Frank McKinney, Real Estate Artist

6X Best-Selling Author

Chapter 3

Getting a Mentor

I could probably write a whole book on this topic, and in one of my other books I talk about forming a "Board of Directors;" people who help you make good decisions, coach and support you. Mentors are critical to achieving success in business, and I would argue, in life as well. The "Board of Directors" concept came out of my early career in the mortgage business, when I was just starting out and the economy had pretty much tanked in 2008.

I knew I needed extra help and support, and I knew that hiring a mentor or coach would be my best bet. But, with the little bit of money that I did have, I also couldn't afford to hire a coach; the least expensive one I could find was $5,000, and I didn't even have $500 to spend. I could have hired this person, if I didn't pay my assistants, but I had made a commitment to them that I would pay them no matter what. Sometimes that meant that I was pulling money out of my credit cards or getting a cash advance. Times were tough.

Instead, I built my own personal "Board of Directors." These were five people that I knew, liked and trusted, and who I knew would be there for me. We would get together on a regular basis and talk about the problems we were having, challenges we were facing, and successes we were experiencing. We would give each other unbiased opinions on different solutions and ideas. They were going through similar difficulties as I was, and we all shared ideas and brainstormed solutions that we were all bound to experience at one point or another.

This was almost like a mastermind group of people that I could trust, and it didn't cost anybody anything to be in the group. We would just go for coffee and talk. Two of the original members of this group were my very good friend and his wife, who was one of my top clients. Sometimes we wouldn't even talk about business issues; we would cover personal experiences as well in order to help shape each other to be better people.

One of my first Board of Director members was Lex Levinrad, who first taught me how to invest in real estate. I bought my first investment property, right after the crash for $12,500, from Lex's advice. I got a loan for $25,000 to purchase this house, so that I could use the extra proceeds as I dug myself out of the financial hole that I was in. That house was easily worth 4-5 times the amount I paid, and that's what I ended up getting paid, and then some, by renting it out. I learned the potential of real investment from Lex, and I'm forever grateful for having him on my Board of Directors.

When you consider forming a group like this, you want to find five people who want to see you become successful. They can be colleagues, community members, clients, business partners or friends. They can come from any background or experience level, as the main goal is to share experiences, ideas, and solutions. They need to be positive and uplifting; you don't want to hang out with "Debbie Downers," the fictional character from Saturday Night Live who is negative about everything.

You want to hang out with people who want to see you grow. Likewise, you have to be ready and willing to give to the individuals in your group; with referrals, advice, and support. For example, in my initial group, I was the "connector." If someone said they needed help with a logo design, I connected them with a designer. If someone said they needed an appraiser, I connected them.

Just the other day I got a call from a client whose son is purchasing property, and who wanted me to close the real estate deal. While we were chatting, she said, "I was just looking at my company logo that you helped me out with. Thanks, again for that." Now, I wasn't a graphic designer, but can I give her unbiased opinions on what I think as a potential customer of hers? Sure! I still remember when the group came up with an idea for a logo that we created together that she is still using today - 15 years later.

As you grow the business and are now starting to earn money, you will want to take things to the next level, and this is when a professional mentor can really help out. We're not talking about a mentor that is only to help you build your business, but a mentor who can teach you how to be a better person, how to be a better business owner, and industry professional. Paid mentors can help you learn from their own experiences, and from their mistakes. If you can find a mentor in your field, that's even better.

So many real estate professionals are afraid to network with people who are doing the same thing they are doing, because they're afraid someone will steal their business. But the way I see it, and have experienced it in my career, is that if someone steals your idea or your customers, don't worry; they'll fail. They'll fail because they're not good enough or enough to succeed on their own. So, don't be afraid of this. Living in that type of fear will crush you.

I found my own professional mentor, Bob Burg, almost by accident, 10 years ago. One of my business partners, one of the biggest appraisers in this part of Florida and a member of the BNI group that I belonged to, asked me if I had read a book that she showed me. It was a tiny, red book; a thick pamphlet almost, titled, "The Go-Giver: A Little Story About a Powerful Business Idea." Told in a parable format, it teaches about the value of "giving" over "getting," and is now one of several in a series.

I looked up the author and saw that he lived just 45 minutes away. I sent him an email that said, "I don't even know if this message is going to get to you, but I have a person who literally changed my life by introducing me to a large real estate broker who helped me keep my business alive during these tough times. Anyway, this friend of mine wants to meet you. Would you be open to that?" He quickly wrote back and said, "Absolutely!"

I wasn't even looking for a mentor. I just wanted to help my friend meet the person who wrote an amazing book that helped her. I had messaged him on Friday, bought the book on a Saturday, and read it in one sitting. We drove up, my friend and I, the next day, Sunday morning, to meet Bob. We sat down to chat at a Dunkin Donuts in Jupiter, Florida and talked about the book. He told us about the program that he had created called, "Endless Referrals."

Now, I had no clue about any of Bob's work until that weekend; didn't know about the importance of giving referrals, or the value in emphasizing the laws of value, compensation, influence, authenticity, and receptivity. None of it. But, I was taken by his sincerity, wisdom, experience and common sense ideas. I asked about his program, and was gently told that the investment fee was $5,000. I signed up on the spot.

The real estate market was still struggling and I dug into an even deeper hole. But, this time, with Bob's help and leadership, I had become an Endless Referral Consultant, certified through the Go-Giver organization. I saw this as a side-business but didn't realize that this program was going to change my life. As an Endless Referral Consultant, I could teach the program that he had developed, and sell his books, CD and other program materials. I could travel the country, talking about how to create a referral-based business.

Never once did I charge for these services. I became one of Bob's top students and basically took his program and taught others how to build a referral-based business. A very simple concept. This experience taught me how to network better, how to treat relationships better, how to first be a referral giver instead of a referral receiver. I created endless referrals for my own business, and fast-forward ten years and those endless referrals mean business just comes in. All I have to do is keep my relationships happy and educated, be honest and the business now continues to grow.

Mentors can come into your life before you're even an adult, and their lessons stick with you for years. I never liked school, and when I was in high school, I was enrolled in an alternative program. I was fortunate enough to have a teacher named Jim Hennessey. As part of his program, he gave us all the tools we needed to be successful. I received one-on-one attention from this young teacher, who had just started teaching.

He was about 8 years older than me and was just starting his own adult life. These lessons had nothing to do with the curriculum, and the trivia that is often what substitutes for real schooling; he took me under his wing and took me to his fire department where he was a volunteer. He knew that he needed to build a meaningful relationship with me in order to get me to where I needed to go. He showed me that he had my back; that he was on my side. He coached me and was an incredible influence on me. He made sure I passed the high school graduation test that I had failed three times before.

I think working with a mentor helps with confidence levels, and helps dissuade fears that we can all fall victim to; fears that can halt our moving forward in life and in business. Being around great people who have already succeeded, who have made mistakes and will help you avoid making those same mistakes, helps you learn and grow at a faster pace, I think. I have friends who own title companies, and if one of them calls up and wants to brainstorm ideas, I'm there for them, immediately. I've learned things, and we can all learn lessons from each other in business.

RESCUE YOUR BUSINESS ASSIGNMENT

Make a list of at least 5-7 individuals who might be potential "Board of Directors" members.

1.

2.

3.

4.

5.

6.

7.

What would you offer your "Board of Directors?"

_____

_____

_____

_____

Why do you think a "go-giver" mentality might be more effective than a "go-getter" mentality?

_____

_____

_____

_____

_____

"You can have everything in life you want, if you will just help enough other people get what they want."

Zig Ziglar

Bestselling Author

Chapter 4

Don't be Afraid to Share Your Knowledge

Fear will paralyze you. Guaranteed. In any business, in any relationship. If you give into fear, you will fail. Fear equals failure, plain and simple.

Referral Marketing Mastery (RMM) is a program that I completed some years back. One of the tasks in the program is to find your biggest competitor and learn what they don't know; learn what they're doing that their clients do not like. Learn what's important that they're not doing successfully. Meet with them, learn their challenges.

But, why would another title company, in this case, meet with me and tell me all of their trade secrets, so I would learn how to build a more successful business? Why would they share this information with me? Why would someone who is doing what I'm looking to do, share what they know and have learned? This didn't make sense to me, that a competitor would offer me this type of information, but I went ahead and scheduled a meeting since it was a requirement of the Referral Marketing Mastery program.

At the time, my biggest competitor was another title company that was already established in the real estate broker's office where I was friends with the broker. We met for coffee, with no intention to steal her clients, but simply to learn what she did right and think about how I could do it better. What was she doing wrong? What was she doing right? How could I improve on her strengths, and fill in the gaps of her weaknesses? It was a nice conversation, as I learned from her, asked questions, and shared my own experiences with her as well.

One of the things I took note of was how she didn't build and maintain meaningful relationships that would keep her business self-sustaining. She just wanted "the deal" that came from being inside a real estate broker's space. She didn't build relationships with the real estate agents, didn't add value to the broker's office, and basically sat and waited for the business to come to her.

Eventually, clients of the broker filed some complaints about the sitting title company, and the broker investigated what had gone wrong. She realized that the title company representative wasn't really adding value to the organization as a whole and that the relationships were suffering. In the meantime, I was biding my time, helping out as I could. One time I even helped the real estate broker put together a PowerPoint presentation for a talk with the brokerage office. I worked on building relationships and adding value to the office.

The broker made the decision to ask the title company to leave, and for me to take the role as the primary title company in the office. Not because I asked for it. Not because I undermined the other title company. I had simply learned from that company's mistakes, improved on what they were providing, built meaningful relationships and added value to the office and the agents. I also wasn't afraid to share my knowledge, with no expectation of return in mind.

Share this information with others. What makes you successful? What works for you? How do you create and nurture client relationships? Business relationships? What technology are you using to run your business? All of the things that have helped you succeed, share that information with others, because it will come back to you tenfold. You need to not be afraid to share secrets. You need to not be afraid to share how you run your business.

I think the important piece here is to know that you also don't know it all. You can always learn and improve, and you can learn from others. You also learn so much by teaching others and being generous with your time and energy. But, bottom line, don't be satisfied with what you think you know and understand about building relationships and building your business. This alone, will increase your business and the value that you offer in the field, and in the community.

In sharing this type of knowledge and information, you're building relationships within your field. This will help you survive an economic downturn, or a "blip" in your industry. Instead of worrying about the next deal, worry about the next relationship. Shift your focus from "deal" to "relationship" emphasis, and this can be done, in great part, by sharing your time and your information with others in your own field. These relationships are not about people who can help you earn money; they are about helping someone else. By helping more people, it helps me build a better and bigger business.

When I attend an industry event, sometimes people don't understand why my table is always full where other tables are not. I think, sure, people want to be around successful people. But, more importantly, people want to be around people they know, like and respect. That's what I mean by creating relationships that will eventually give back to you. By sharing that information that you have, you will allow people to get to know you, like you and ultimately trust you. They will send business your way, because you're seen as one of the "good guys." Because you are.

People need to feel that you have their back, if something goes wrong. Are you offering that to your clients? To your potential clients? To your business partners and colleagues? Do they think that you will look out for them if something goes wrong? Do they trust you? Don't run away if something goes wrong. Step in. Step up and fix it. Do your colleagues and clients see this in you?

Most businesses, no matter what they are, are really in the business of problem-solving. The title company's responsibility is to solve problems of title and property ownership, and then guarantee that if that problem pops up, insuring that it won't be a problem. Real estate brokers solve the problem of someone needing to sell their home or property, or someone needing to find property. When done right, these are not businesses that are a mere collection of "deals," they all involve helping people, solving a problem, providing a sense of security and teamwork, and creating relationships.

This chapter really is about fears. If you're reading this point , and your fears are overwhelming you, you need to close this book, send it to me, and I'll send you your money back. I know that you will not succeed if you are afraid to take the steps that I'm outlining for you here. So, I'll say it again; don't be afraid to share your knowledge with others.

Fear = Failure. Don't talk or think poorly about your competitor. The bottom line is there is plenty of business to go around if you show people that you can be trusted and that you give more than you take. Thrive with your competitor. I love to hear stories of other title companies closing a tricky deal. It's great!

RESCUE YOUR BUSINESS ASSIGNMENT

What are some of the fears that you have about your business?

_____

_____

_____

How can you put those fears away, so that you can open yourself up to building relationships in your business and industry?

_____

_____

_____

What else might be blocking you from succeeding, and sharing information freely with others?

_____

_____

_____

"Being a leader involves more than just standing at the front of the line."

John Di Lemme

Strategic Business Coach Champions

Chapter 5

Proper Planning for a Stormy Day

The recession of 2008 hit me hard; it almost killed my business, but I learned from many mistakes that I made. This is one of the biggest lessons, that I learned the hard way. I was about $750,000 in debt, closing three deals a month, writing pay checks out of my credit card cash advance.

Those days were tough, when I would go to the bank and cash an advance check so that I could pay my staff. I never once touched the escrow account; that wasn't my money, and too many people have been burned by title companies dipping into escrow accounts, illegally.

There will be another recession; another economic downturn. It's not "if," but when...

The first year I moved to Florida, in 2001, I earned $60,000 in the mortgage brokerage business; I blew it all. Recently married, I spent all those earnings just getting established, and trying to survive in my new home state. In 2002, I made another $60,000 and increased that to $90,000 in 2003. Things were great - I would close upwards of $30,000 a month in deals, and my income kept going up and up and up.

I partnered with some other brokers, and we opened an office with marble floors and all the other luxuries of a nice office. My desk alone cost $5,000; it was like we were printing money in the business at the time. Until it crashed. Overnight.

It wasn't like I went from 30 deals to 29 to 26 deals. I literally went from 30 deals a month to 3 deals. People weren't closing, loans got denied and I lost everything I had. All those business partners that were in our fancy offices bailed on the lease, leaving me to figure that out on my own. I just paid whatever I could possibly pay to the landlord, begging him to let me stay in the building so I could try to rescue *my* business.

Bringing in these partners, assuming they would support me and my business, was probably the biggest mistake I made in business. I didn't select the right partners, ones that were going to share in my vision and goals; partners who would celebrate successes and stick with me through difficult times.

You need to plan for stormy days; that economic downturn of 2008 and 2009 hit me hard, just like it hit so many people. It tore apart my family. It tore apart my business. It tore apart me, as a person. I didn't know what to do to survive. I don't have a college education; I went from high school to my first career. I knew I always wanted be the best at anything I tried. I would blow everyone out of the water; not in a negative way, but in a positive way. I would do the best that I could do to excel at whatever business I was in, so I knew I could turn this around. I didn't give up, and as I've talked about already, I re-started, built better relationships, and started re-growing over the next few years.

Things went back up to 20, 30, 50, 60 deals a month. I would set realistic goals; for example, I would set an annual goal to increase my monthly closings by 5. In other words, if this year I was closing 25 deals monthly, I would set my goal for the next year to close 30 deals monthly. Month after month. And, increase that goal by 5 every year; year after year. Most of the time, I was able to exceed those goals, because the referrals were growing, and the relationships were building.

Another important lesson I learned was to not have any debt. For many years, I didn't even have a credit card. If I didn't have the cash in my pocket, I didn't spend it. Living within my means, and with the income I had and cash immediately available to me, helped me prepare for any other economic downturns that hit, and might hit in the future. The building that we're in now, we purchased without any debt. That way, when the market crashes, if I have to throttle back on some of my staff because we don't have enough deals, as sad as that would be, it means, that we can stay in business. Without a big rent expense or mortgage, low overhead and no credit card bills to pay, we would be able to survive, professionally and personally in tough economic times.

If you don't plan for a stormy day, when that storm hits you may be stuck, and out of business. How many real estate agents and mortgage brokers all went out of business when that crash of 2008 hit? Some people ask me how much debt is too much, or what percentage of their income is reasonable to hold in debt? My answer is simple. I don't believe in debt, including mortgaging your house. I don't care if it's tax-deductible, or if you can write off the interest; because WHEN the storm comes, you will not be able to maintain that debt.

Other advice that I give business owners who consult with me is to not sign for anything personally. That can be the takedown for you. Be careful with personal guarantees; this was a tough lesson for me as well, my original business partners and I personally guaranteed our lease for that big, fancy office space. Even though my mother warned me not to sign the lease personally, I did anyway. Whoever thought that the business would slow down and come to a screaming halt like that. I ended up owning that debt.

I make sure that I have six months of reserves or savings that are immediately available to me in the case of a downturn. This goes for personal and business expenses. If you keep your monthly expenses low, you'd be surprised how easily you can manage this; but the key is keeping that low overhead, with little to no debt in your personal and business portfolio. You should know how much, exactly, you need to bring in every month just to pay the bills.

If you've never studied the work of financial guru, Dave Ramsey, now's the time to understand his model for living life debt-free and being able to ride any economic wave, good or bad, that will hit during your lifetime. I learned these strategies the hard way, and you don't have to. If you're bringing in great money now, awesome. But it will blow up eventually. Something will happen that will disrupt your current income. If you plan accordingly, it can just be a speed bump, instead of something that can destroy your life.

Life isn't about "get rich, quick." But, it is about being able to pay for your children's' college, your retirement, vacations, a nice house and cars. I'm not rich; but, I have a great family, I don't have any debt, I have a nice business with 15 employees who all go home to their families and pay their bills, and it's fulfilling.

There are small baby steps that you can take in your business to help you survive the next crash. And, if you can survive tough economic times, you can be very successful.

Play things smart and slow; that protects your dream. Avoid costly mistakes like high debt, signing off personally for business expenses and financial responsibilities, and renting the big, fancy office with marble floors.

You need to keep your expenses as low as possible, and run the best, most honest business you can. I sometimes drive my employees crazy by tracking down a discrepancy of a couple of dollars on a transaction, and taking hours to find out who that money belongs to. It's not my money, it's your money, I think to myself. But, that kind of honesty, and that kind of integrity gets out in the world, and you'll find people will give you their money and business. They don't care about those marble floors as much as they care that they feel that you're taking good care of them. That you're honest. That you're one of the "good guys."

If you don't save for a rainy day, when that rainy day comes, it will wipe you out. I recommend different "piggy banks," to accomplish this. Something I did years ago would be to take a specific portion of a sale, or income, and set it aside immediately. For example, if I had a $10,000 sale, I would take $2,000 of that and blow it on whatever I wanted. The rest, I made sure that I put it away toward my six-months of reserves. Again, that includes reserves for personal as well as business expenses.

"Desperate people do desperate things" was a saying my father-in-law Ken used and Alana continues. If you haven't prepared for the rain day, you end up doing desperate things. No one wants to do business with someone who is desperate, which just makes your situation even more desperate. I often quote one of my mentors and friend David Dweck that "Florida is a sunny place with some shady characters". But, that's what happens; people end up ripping other people off, and ruining lives.

RESCUE YOUR BUSINESS ASSIGNMENT

What are your monthly personal expenses?

_____

_____

_____

Business expenses?

_____

_____

_____

How much a month do you pay in debt?

_____

_____

Look at your income and expenses and find money that you can save every month. How are you going to do that by either reducing debt or expenses and/or increasing your income?

_____

_____

_____

"You are not stuck. You can change. You just need to make the decision to do it! Others have done it before you and you can too. But it starts with a single thought in your head that says; 'I can do this'"

Lex Levinrad

Real Estate Investor, Speaker & Mentor

Chapter 6

Road to Financial Freedom

After you've planned for the stormy day, discussed in the previous chapter, you need to create your success platform toward financial freedom. What I mean by "financial freedom" is to make sure that you have enough income coming in to cover your expenses. Continue this plan, until you could stop working tomorrow, but still have income coming in, for the rest of your life, to continue to cover those expenses.

For example, I invest in private loans for people purchasing real estate. You could purchase houses and have rental income. Others have properties that they can rent out as vacation properties or other income sources. All of these should lead you toward a healthy and happy, fulfilling retirement. Start developing the three F's: Financial Freedom Funnels.

These funnels are basically saying that you have one funnel that generates a certain amount of income, then another funnel that generates a different kind of income, and maybe even a third funnel. What happens if one of these funnels dries up? No problem! You have two others that generate income for you, and you can either start a new funnel, or repair and rebuild the funnel that failed on you. By developing multiple streams of income, and not putting all your proverbial eggs in one basket, you have back-up plans to help you out if something hits that wipes one of your income streams out.

A major way to financial freedom is owning your house with no mortgage; then the only thing you have to worry about are taxes and insurances which are due once or twice a year. After that tax payment is made, or the insurance payment, I don't have to worry about the financial obligation of paying a mortgage month after month after month. I have another year before I have to make a payment "on the house."

Saving for your kid's college is another way toward financial freedom. Not only are you preparing for a heavy financial hit when your child hits his or her college years, you are also helping them with their future financial freedom by making sure they don't need to go into debt to get a college education.

Consider an investment, IRA, 401k or other savings account where you can create financial freedom toward your retirement. Build it slowly. Set up an auto-draft in to your savings account, a money market account, and other financial tools. Let the compounding interest work for you, and sleep well at night knowing that you are building a strong safety net.

I don't look at my monthly brokerage statement. I don't care what it is giving me on a monthly basis. I'm looking at 20, 30, 40 years from now, and planning for the long-term. By adding money, every month, I know that I am building a future of financial stability and total financial freedom for my family. Set it and forget it! Properly planning and saving today will help prevent problems tomorrow.

You don't have to work until you're 80, and never really enjoy life. My grandfather came from very poor roots in Cuba, and built a very successful textile business, retired early and lived his life fully. He would take my grandmother on yearly cruises. They would go dancing together and spend amazing time with friends. They enjoyed life in the very fullest, for many, many years. Before he passed away a couple of years ago, I got a chance to sit down with him for two weeks, and he shared with me his ideas to make sure his family was taken care of. By no means was he rich or wealthy. He didn't have a mortgage. He didn't have credit cards. He didn't have any debt. He made sure that every single month he had enough money coming in to enjoy his retirement.

I don't want to be the richest person in the world. I want to be comfortable, for as long as I live. And, I want to make sure that things are set up in my family so that if something happens to me, my family will be ok, because I've set aside money, secured their future with life insurance policies, and paid for their schooling long before they were old enough to go to college. I want to be able to retire comfortably.

In my opinion the best way to start building passive income would be to stay away from "get rich quick" schemes like MLM, or multi-level-marketing businesses. Yes, you can be very successful, but there is a very small percentage of people who can be successful within the MLM model.

If the vast majority of your income from an "investment" like this comes from getting more people to sign up to "sell" the product or service, versus income generated from the actual sale of that product or service, you are in an MLM scam, and your chances of succeeding are slim to none.

Use the money you make in your business to make money elsewhere. Develop multiple income funnels, and if you save money to put away for your retirement, or your children's' college, don't touch that money! Even if you "need" it, struggle, and find a way to get by without touching that money.

Most Realtors that I know do not have a retirement plan, nor the income to get there. They might be struggling to pay their monthly bills because they've acquired more debt than they can handle. I'm hoping to help out my friends in the real estate industry by giving and sharing ideas to help save up, live debt free, and enjoy an early retirement.

For example, most Americans have saved less than $10,000 for retirement. Almost 10% of seniors are declaring bankruptcy, and that number is bound to increase. Nearly one-third of retirees are going into retirement with mortgage debt. Are you one of the over 50% of Americans that report losing sleep because they're worried about retirement? Don't be. Don't let yourself be a "victim." Take charge of your financial freedom and start today!

RESCUE YOUR BUSINESS ASSIGNMENT

Determine your level of expendable income - income left over after all the expenses are paid - and determine at least three different savings vehicles or accounts. What is that amount, and which accounts will you set up? (Retirement? College? Home purchase?)

_____

_____

_____

_____

Set up direct deposit accounts for your savings vehicles. How much will you deposit into each account? List them separately, here:

_____

_____

_____

_____

_____

_____

_____

_____

"Success is in the moment; so make every moment count."

Omar Periu

Master Motivational Teacher

Chapter 7

Set Yourself Apart from Your Competition

It doesn't matter what business you're in, there will always be competition. In real estate, it doesn't matter if you're a Realtor, mortgage broker, investor, or title company; you will have competition. Sometimes it seems that there's a title company on every corner, or a mortgage broker, or Realtor on every block. However, this is no reason to feel intimidated.

If you live in fear, your competitor will take you out. They will do something better than you. They will take more risks and put themselves out there; setting you up for failure. Don't let them do this to you. You need to set yourself apart from your competition. Find out what that needs to be in your local business area; what are your competitors not providing that you can? Are they pricing themselves out of the market? Are they not offering quality customer service? Are they not standing behind their word? Are they not honest?

For me, and my title company, what I decided to do was to move away from a "make the deal" mentality into developing meaningful and real relationships in the community. For me, that turned into real results and helped me grow my company to where it is now. This is how I set myself apart from my competition, because all my competitors, at networking events, are constantly asking for business, searching out the deal. They seem desperate to me, and I think that plays off to the consumer, as well.

Instead of asking for the next deal at networking events, I just try to get to know other people. What are their interests? What do they do in their spare time? How did they find themselves in Florida, or in the real estate industry? I simply want to get to know them, and turn that relationship, organically, into a referral opportunity.

I don't start the conversation with this expectation in mind. I just start the conversation, with no expectation, and see where it goes from there. If I am being true to myself, and honest with the other person, very often it turns into business for me. So, the way I set myself apart from my competition is by offering honest relationships and a helping hand in the community.

How can a Realtor or mortgage broker or title company set themselves apart from the competition? The first step is to find out what is needed in the marketplace; what can you offer that is different from anyone else in the area? For example, a real estate investor can set themselves apart from the competition by never cutting corners and always working on the important parts of the house; the kitchen and the bathrooms should have the wow factor. Why? Because, who's walking in and making the decision most of the time? Usually the wife, and if the wife loves the house, the husband will often agree. That's the reality; women make upwards of 85% of all purchasing decisions, including the home purchase.

As an investor, or home builder, if you do this consistently, you'll be known as someone who builds or rehabs an amazing house. You, also have to stand behind all your construction and/or improvements. If something goes wrong, don't hesitate and waver; put in the time and money needed to make things right. Build trust with the end-consumer, and you will also build trust with the Realtors, mortgage brokers, title companies, and everyone else involved in the real estate transaction. You will be known as an honest real estate investor; and, that reputation is priceless.

The real estate brokerage office that I've been affiliated with, Charles Rutenberg Realty for many, many years, is a rock in the community. Its history started with a very well know builder from the west coast of Florida. Everybody knew about this builder, and they knew his homes when they saw one. They knew it on sight because of a consistency in design and quality, and a stellar reputation. The homes were built to the highest standards, and people loved their homes.

Realtors can set themselves apart from the competition in a variety of ways, as well. Don't be the type of Realtor who thinks that all you need to do is take someone to a house, and it will sell. Instead, invest time in learning about the house, preview it, ask questions of the sellers, make sure that when you take a client to a house, you're at the top of your game. Know the school district, know the ratings of the schools, show them where the schools are, for example.

You have to earn your 3% commission; the days are over when you could just pull up to a house, open the door, show people around, and write up a contract. There is so much more involved in every real estate transaction, and so much competition, you really have to stand apart. What's a unique product or service that you can offer, that no one else is providing in your area?

Get to know your clients! How many people reading this book right now actually interview their clients to find out what their needs are? Or do they just accept that all a client needs is a certain number of bedrooms, bathrooms, and a pool? Why do they want a pool? Do they have children? Do they want to be able to see the children from the kitchen window while the kids play in the pool?

Just recently, my mother told me a story about when we were children. Neighborhood kids would come over to swim in our pool. She told me that if she had to go to the bathroom, she would make every kid get out of the pool, walk into the house, and lock every door and padlock the pool gate. She wanted to make sure all the kids were safe.

Learn what's important to the client. Would they tell you a story like my mom told me? If they're asking for a pool in the backyard, is it easily monitored from inside the house? Is it separately fenced? Is that what your client is looking for? Because, if they want a gate around the pool, separate from the yard enclosure, and you show them a house that doesn't have that safety feature, the client will think you don't value their needs, or them.

Let's say you have an ideal home in mind, but there is no separate gate around the pool. Then do the research on how much it would cost to put in a fence and a gate, so the buyer knows you're thinking about them, and that you've done your homework. They can then factor that in when they're making a decision. A really common mistake that Realtors make is not truly personalizing the home shopping experience. If you don't do this, your competition will out-sell you, every time. Selling a house is easy; selling an experience is difficult. If you sell an experience, you will automatically generate referrals from that client, and clients to come.

Selling an experience is difficult to learn. When I used to sell houses as a Realtor, I used to do this. I would sell the house, only after doing tons of research on what the client needed and prioritized, what the neighborhood offered, minute details about the homes that I was taking them to. I did all the homework so that the buyer didn't have to. Many times, I would sell a house on the first showing of that house.

I knew exactly what they wanted; what colors they liked, where they wanted to take their kids the school, the amenities that they were looking for. Do they want the kids' bedrooms near the master bedroom, or away from the master suite? If they wanted a nursery room near the master bedroom, I wasn't going to show them a split-level house; I showed them a house where the nursery room was near the master bedroom.

By asking the client questions, you can solve problems for them; by solving problems, personalizing it, you are setting yourself apart from the competition. You can then sell more houses.

Mortgage brokers and lenders can do the same thing; learn about what the client's finances are, and what they can really afford. Do they need help patching up their credit rating? If so, maybe a 2 year ARM can help them get into a house, and they can refinance after they get things cleaned up. Find out what their long-term goals are. Maybe you can sell them an ARM because they have short-term goals; maybe a fixed-rate would work better for them.

Show your customers how they can pay off their loan sooner, by adding extra principal payments, so that when they sell their house, they have more equity than they would have had normally. With my mortgage broker clients, I would put all of their debt on a spreadsheet, and show them how much their mortgage payment is, how much money they needed to pay for their house, how much debt they could pay off, and how much money was left over. I would then teach them how to then take that money and invest it into something smart; for retirement, for college funds, and for additional income potential.

Those clients that came to me $30,000 or $40,000 in debt, and who needed to refinance their house, I would show them how to not spend money they didn't need to spend; to help them get out of destructive debt loads, for good. So, when I would show them that I could save them $500 a month, for example, by refinancing their home, I would show them what they could do with that $500 a month to save for their future, and for a rainy day; to be smart with that extra money.

What kind of mortgage broker would coach their client on long-term financial planning; helping them understand how they can pay down their debt, improve their credit rating, and spend what they can afford? Not many do. That's selling an experience, and not just a mortgage. That's creating a repeat customer, and a referral network. Taking the time to give to your clients, above and beyond, will set you apart from your competition. Solve your clients' problems. Do something that your competition might be afraid to do. Care more than your competition does about that relationship with the client. Building that relationship meant that the client would call me back for another transaction or ask if I could help a friend or family member. I can then help solve their problems, and they know I have their back. For example, I respond to client emails and messages as quickly as possible, so they know I have their back...NOW! That builds trust.

After the crash of 2008 and 2009, this type of strategy helped me survive through those tough markets. After 2010, when things started to pick up again, this way of doing business helped me recover much more quickly than my competition. I never looked back. It wasn't always this way; before I learned to invest in relationships, I was notified by my mortgage broker partner that mortgage companies didn't want to use me for my title services. I learned the hard way that they went and used someone else who took better care of those relationships.

Set yourself apart from the competition and set your standards higher than the competition. Do something different, because being different gets attention, and that attention gets you more business. Help people identify and solve their problems. When you help people get through their problems, you become a referral marketing master. When you're a referral marketing master, your clients won't want to work with anybody but you, and they'll make sure everybody knows it. Because you know your stuff and you have their back!

RESCUE YOUR BUSINESS ASSIGNMENT

In your research of your competition, what are they NOT doing that you can do to set yourself apart?

_____

_____

_____

_____

_____

How can you personalize your client experience in order to show that you know your stuff, and that you truly care about your clients?

_____

_____

_____

_____

_____

"People don't care how much you know until they know how much you care."

Ivan Misner

NY Times Bestselling Author and Founder of BNI

Chapter 8

Become a Master at What You Do

My nickname in the title insurance industry is "The Title King". They say there is nobody better than me, or maybe I'm just doing something right.

I think becoming a master in anything that you do is really important. So, whether I was installing carpet and tile, delivering pizza or being a firefighter. Whatever industry I'm working in, from just after of high school, to now, I've always strived to be the very best that I can be.

When I was the Director of Fire Safety and Security at the Crowne Plaza Hotel in Manhattan, New York, we had 48 floors to take care of, including stand-pipe system, sprinkler systems, stairwells, fire extinguishers, and more. When I started there, it became obvious to me that there was not one person on the team that knew all the information needed to ensure the safety of our guests in the case of fire and other safety issues.

I took it upon myself to learn everything about the sprinkler systems, where every stairwell led, where every fire extinguisher was located, and how everything worked. I learned exactly how everything was connected, every evacuation route, the construction of the sprinkler system. Everything. It was important for me to master the system and know it inside and out. I felt that it was my job.

This carries on to my entire life. I've always felt that it's critical that I master whatever I am working at. I think it's important for anyone working in the real estate industry, whether you're a Realtor, a lender, a mortgage broker, or a title agent. It doesn't matter what your field is. You need to master whatever you are doing. It's not just a requirement if you own your own company; I didn't own that hotel, but you can bet that I knew that fire safety system inside and out.

This isn't tied to pay grade - I didn't get paid more at the hotel for learning what I learned. But I truly felt, and still feel, that if I'm being paid to do something, it's my job to master that task, and give my employer the very best that I can. Does it eventually lead to higher pay? Usually. And, if it doesn't, it almost certainly leads to healthy relationships, and future opportunities that I might not even have even had in my view.

My mother was a workaholic for many years, so maybe this is where I got this attitude from. She always mastered the skill set of whatever her job was. She saw it as her job to build the owner's business. Now, I own my own businesses, so my job is to build my business. But, again, many people work for other companies, so it's not just about being a business owner. It's about being a master at what you do.

You should be able to teach what you know; that's how you become master. If you can't teach someone how to do your job, you will never become a master at what you do. Once you start to become a teacher, you start to become a master. Once you start to become a master, you start generating that reach to the community to be known as a person who is an expert in what you do.

That's a challenge here in the South Florida real estate market. I see so many practitioners who are not a master at what they do. They don't really understand what their task is; it's so important for them to take a step back and learn the business. Learn what the Realtors are looking for, learn what the consumers are looking for; learn what they want. When you do this, you will reap the rewards and benefits in profits showing on your bottom line.

In establishing this reputation as a master in our industry, for example, at every event we attend, the questions come right to us. Because we know the answers. We have attendees who have side-stepped asking questions to the real estate lawyers and asked us instead. They know that if they go to the attorney table, they'll get some legal jargon that will make their head spin. I know this, too - sometimes I'll take the same question and ask two or three different attorneys that question. I'll get two or three different answers.

When thinking about what you need to know to become a master, start at the end result or goal. For example, at the hotel, the end result would be to make sure that everyone got out safely in the case of a fire or other catastrophic event. What do I need to know to make that happen? I need to know every stairwell, every fire exit, every evacuation route; and to make sure that every staff member knows their area as well.

If I know how to get to the end result, and you ask me a question about that, I'll be able to give you a simple, straightforward answer. Because, I've done the work to figure it out already, for you. At the same time, it's important to understand how things apply to different cases. There are rarely black and white answers, so you have to master understanding all sides of the situation.

What drives me to become the master of my trade? This goes back to working just out of high school. As an ethical person, it felt to me that if I was getting paid to do something, I needed to do it the best I could. In order to do that, I needed to learn everything I needed to know about what I did, and how things worked in the system of where I was working. My job, no matter what it was, depended on me knowing and owning my stuff. My job is to do what I'm being paid to do, and to do it the best that I can.

So many people just want to get by. They just want to get their pay check. They just want to close the deal and get paid; they don't want to do it to the best of their ability. That, in my opinion, is where they fail. If there was something that I didn't do in my job, it was because I couldn't, not because I wouldn't. In my business, I continue to build my mastery skills, I read tons of case studies, so that I learn what's going on in the industry. I read up on new trends and technology; how can I stay ahead of my competition? For example, we were the first title company approved in the State of Florida to do a fully electronic closing!

By mastering your job and industry, you stay ahead of the curve. Life is a series of sharp curves, so you need to be able to stay ahead and master that, because otherwise someone else is going to do it, and do it better than you. Real estate agents, for example, need to understand, the contract that their clients sign inside and out. They need to understand the school districts, zoning laws, utility providers, HOAs and everything else that would be important to your client. You have to be able to hold your client's hand so that they have the best possible experience - again, remember, you are selling the experience, not the house.

I think a lot of successful Realtors focus their efforts on particular markets or areas. Maybe one Realtor specializes in vacant and rural land properties. Maybe another on the east half of a county. Maybe a third Realtor specializes in helping families with children find the best home match for all their needs. This specialization is a form of mastery in the real estate brokerage business. This just makes sense, too. A Realtor can't possibly know everything about everything in every city or location in a county. You just can't. However, they can know everything about their particular niche.

For example, in the development where I live, there is a Realtor named Kate. She is the master of anything and everything about my development. If there is a house for sale in the development, she knows about it and knows it inside and out. She knows what's going on in the Homeowner's Association, including proposed projects, association amenities, and more. She is a resource for real estate professionals who are completing a deal within the development. I know I'd send clients to her, if they are looking for something within it! She's a master in our neighbourhood.

In this part of Florida, we have a lot of homeowners and condo associations. If a Realtor is working in an area like this, they need to know every development association dues, and what's included in those dues. For example, some developments include cable in the dues, or water, or golf fees. If they don't know this information, they are not serving their clients, and they are not being masters of their field. If they're not a master of the area, someone else will come in and run circles around them.

A successful Realtor should easily pull in a six-figure income; those are your masters. Realtors who are not committed to mastering their profession, will average around $45,000-60,000 a year in our area. Not bad, right? But, certainly not at a mastery level. That six-figure income potential only comes when the real estate professional has committed the time and energy to become a master of whatever their job is in the business.

My entire career path came from this sense of mastery. When I first started in the business, I was a mortgage broker, and I became frustrated because the real estate "professionals" I was working with were not masters at their craft. So, I got my real estate license so that I could become an expert in the real estate agent business. Then, I started dealing with sub-par title companies, and you can guess what I did next. I got three licenses so that I could understand and help solve problems in almost every aspect of the real estate industry. I did it because I was getting blamed for the mistakes of others, and I figured that if I was going to get blamed for a mistake, it should be because it was my own mistake, versus someone else's.

So, I would have a client and help them find a house, get a loan, get clean title, and then homeowners insurance (yes, I got a license in that too, eventually). That client will have the best experience they can, because I knew that I was a master at each stage of the real estate transaction. I wasn't worried about a mistake that someone else made, coming back to bite me. I wasn't going to make the same mistakes, and as many mistakes as I saw happening in almost every single real estate transaction. Not that I'm perfect, by any stretch, but when I took that direction, less mistakes were made, and if they were made I knew how to fix them.

Eventually, I focused my efforts to the closing, or title agency aspect, because I realized that as the business started to grow, I couldn't be a master of everything. Even though I only focus on title insurance now, my previous experience helps me understand the transaction from beginning to end, so that I can provide the customer the best experience that I can within the real estate transaction. That previous experience allows me to provide the best possible experience that I can to my client. I know the deal from the real estate agent perspective, from the lender perspective, from the insurance perspective. All that combined, makes me a master.

To succeed in any business, including real estate, you must invest a lot of time to learn and earn. I see so many "get rich quick" schemes, especially on the investor side of things, and they rarely lead to sustained success. So, don't think that attending a weekend workshop makes you an expert. Same as being a licensed Realtor doesn't guarantee success in that field, either. Much time, money and hard work need to be invested before you can become successful on a consistent basis.

What I like to do on the title company's side of things, is go above and beyond. What I think makes me best in the industry is to help support and educate other real estate professionals. I never charge for these services, because again, I'm interested in building relationships. I like to be able to say to any real estate professional who is working with me on a deal, "How can we work this deal together - how can we help each other out?" So, I do a lot of support and education for real estate professionals in my region. For example, I can help explain the real estate contract, or how financing works and what lenders need to see.

It's a rocky road, this real estate business. But I love to help others and carry them along that rocky road to make sure that everyone succeeds. Each person involved in the real estate deal, from the seller, to the buyer, the Realtor to the mortgage broker, should come out better than when they came in. And, then the next deal gets easier. I'm all for motivated newbies, and bringing them into this fun and challenging business.

Build your skills slowly and deliberately. For example, on the investment side, start with just wholesaling properties, maybe getting up to 2-3 a month. Then, if you want, as you've mastered that first stage, rehab one property a quarter. From there, maybe build things up to investing in a rental property, once a year. You can build your mastery portfolio slowly, deliberately, and only progress as you're ready to go to the next level. Don't rush things. There is no shortcut to becoming a master in your field. Dedicate yourself fully and you should be able to become a master in a specialty in your industry in about a year. That will be well worth the time and energy when you start generating endless referrals because people will see you as an expert.

I find motivation by watching YouTube videos related to what I'm trying to learn. I'm not much of a reader, or a TV viewer. Podcasts can be helpful, but for me I prefer short 5-10 minute blurbs that can help me understand a new skill or get motivated to try something new. I get inspired by those who have come before me, and I love to learn things from them. In today's world of social media this gets easier, and with my admittedly short attention span, I can gain more from a 10 minute TED talk than a weekend workshop.

Once you become a master, that doesn't mean you stop learning. The industry changes, technology changes, new opportunities arise, and others fade away. Once you are a master, you are still not finished. Once you think you know it all, if you stop continuing to learn, you will be out of business before you know it. You must continually sharpen the tools in your toolbox to continue to learn and evolve.

RESCUE YOUR BUSINESS ASSIGNMENT

What are you good at?

_____

_____

_____

Where do you need to improve?

_____

_____

_____

Is there an area where you can specialize? List a few, and plot a possible mastery plan for 2-3 specializations

_____

_____

_____

_____

_____

_____

"Success is showing up and making a commitment."

David Dweck

Realtor and Investor

Boca Real Estate Investment Club

Chapter 9

Ask for Testimonials

You've done this, I'm sure. You're online and you're about to purchase something, or you are comparison shopping, so you check the reviews. Maybe you're looking for a good restaurant in the town that you're visiting. Or maybe you're comparing tire shops in your area. Reviews like this speak to the power of testimonials.

How many times have you been about to purchase a product or service, and then seen several negative reviews, so you change your mind? Or you're looking into a service, and you can't find any reviews, so you go onto the next service listing that does have reviews. Testimonials are extremely effective when it comes to increasing your credibility and visibility in your industry and region.

We always ask for testimonials, which is different than asking for referrals. Both of these are important to growing and sharing your business, as long as they're positive! You don't want to share a negative testimonial but you should still learn from it and will want to professionally deal with any negative reviews that might pop up online. I always look on Facebook and Google before I call up any business; that's the first place I go. I want to see testimonials from their clients. I make sure they have more than two or three, and I want to make sure they're not anonymous testimonials, but that they're actual client testimonials.

An acronym that I work with and teach is REFERRAL.

R - Request the Referral or Testimonial
E - Empower Yourself to Only Work with People Who Like to Work with You
F - Focus on the Magic Words that Get Referrals
E - Establish a Powerful Set of Boundaries and Communicate Them Clearly
R - Resolve to Make No More Excuses
R - Run Your Business as if What Others Think About You Makes No Difference
A - Advise Your Clients Without Ever Compromising Your Integrity
L - Love to Help with an Open Heart Even When Your Client's Heart is Closed

REQUEST THE REFERRAL OR TESTIMONIAL

Asking for testimonials or referral is one of the primary functions of your business; you have to do this if you want to survive and thrive. Every single transaction that you have with your client should include the end goal to be able to ask that client for a referral and/or a testimonial. This will ensure that the client has a great experience, so that they can tell others, and share that with you on your website, advertising and other marketing tools.

This is why so many companies, successful companies, have people checking in on Facebook, Google, Yelp and other review sites. When a negative review shows up, you have to deal with it right then and there, professionally and apologetically, while educating that client, and future clients. You've seen this online, I'm sure. You're perusing a business review page, and you see a negative review. Does the owner or manager of that business show up and respond to that negative review? Do they do it in a negative way or a positive way? If done correctly, a negative review can actually bring in business if that business owner handles it the right way.

In order to get testimonials and positive reviews, you have to ask for them. Don't expect your clients to automatically do this for you. Even if they have the best intentions, they usually won't unless there is a direct ask. So, always request a referral.

EMPOWER YOURSELF TO ONLY WORK WITH PEOPLE WHO LIKE TO WORK WITH YOU

Sometimes a potential client, whether it's a consumer or another business, is just not a good fit. You have to be able to turn clients away. If you're a Realtor, you have to be able to know when a buyer or seller just isn't going to work well with you; maybe they're too needy or too demanding, so they'll never be satisfied with your services. Work with people who want to work with you. You are the service provider. Don't take every deal and don't be afraid to turn a deal down.

Now, that's hard to say at the beginning. How do you turn down a deal when you really need the money? But, it's important to understand that you want to work with people who will appreciate your efforts, who want to work with you, and who will make it possible for you to give them a great experience. When a client wants to work with me, I want to work with them, because giver's gain.

FOCUS ON THE MAGIC WORDS THAT GET REFERRALS

You have to focus on asking people for referrals, specifically words that speak to their experience. For example, "Tell me the experience you had; How did it go?" or "Why did you select us again?" Those magic words are going to get you more referrals in the end, plain and simple. But you have to ask how was your experience? Every person is going to have a different perspective on why they like your services. Maybe that reason is you, and your presence in the business. Maybe it's a staff member that was really helpful. Maybe it's because they know we are honest, and we will protect their investment.

As you get testimonials, you'll soon see what clients see as the benefits of doing business with you. You can then use those words in every marketing tool you have, from banner ads, to three-fold brochures, from website pages to presentations that you make. "Here are the benefits of doing business with us," you can proclaim, because your clients have told you. Our clients don't only become a great source of referrals, but also of ideas on how to market our business.

ESTABLISH A POWERFUL SET OF BOUNDARIES AND COMMUNICATE THEM CLEARLY

It's critical to set clear boundaries and communicate those with your clients, so that you're not getting phone calls at 10:00 at night. Set a clear boundary for timelines; we set this up on day one when we get a contract with a client. Here's what to expect, here's how long it will take, here's what could go wrong, here are the steps we'll take.

I tell Realtors all the time that when they get a contract, put that contract in a folder, put important dates in a Google calendar with alerts 24-48 hours before certain important timelines are coming up. When is the loan contingency due? When is the inspection period? When is title due back? Etc.

Follow these timelines and set these boundaries; communicate them with the client so they know what to look for and what to expect. No one likes surprises, so don't be a source of any. If you do this in advance, they won't be calling you every day asking about when the appraisal is, or when is the home inspection. They'll have it all there, clearly and concisely. It's an added service that will give them a great experience. Take that client from contract to closing, as smoothly as you can.

Recently one of my clients took the buyers forfeited $5,000 deposit because their Realtor did not clearly communicate the timeline and missed an important deadline. You don't want to cause that for your clients; you'll have a hard time building a business once you establish that as your reputation. Understand the timeline of each transaction, communicate it clearly, and be a problem-solver, not a problem-maker.

RESOLVE TO MAKE NO MORE EXCUSES

If there is a mistake made and it's your fault, take ownership of that mistake. If a mistake is made by another professional in the transaction, take ownership of your part of that. For example, did you inform your client of the inspection period? Even if that ball was dropped on someone else's part, did you do everything you could to make sure that the inspection happened within the allotted time-frame? If you didn't, take ownership of that.

This sometimes means you have to write a check. It's easy to make an excuse, but that doesn't solve the problem, and it doesn't make the client experience a good one. I think that goes with any business. Don't make excuses, make solutions. Correct any mistake and move forward. If we mess up in our business, we own it. If that means I have to call one of my vendors to rush an order, and I have to pay extra for it, that's fine. That's how you do business. Get it done and get it done quick, without it hurting your client.

RUN YOUR BUSINESS AS IF WHAT OTHERS THINK ABOUT YOU MAKES NO DIFFERENCE

Stop worrying about what everyone else thinks about you. I don't care about what other companies think about us. Do you think we get the best comments from other title companies? No!

Just the other day we had a meeting where another title company's employee totally bashed us in front of an entire group. "After Kevin over-charges you for another closing, you'll want to come to me," she stood up and said.

This was especially silly because we have the best rates in the State of Florida. We have wholesale pricing, because we do around 100 deals a month. But, I know where this came from, and it came from a place of fear. This person lives in fear, and now she tries to discredit our business to make herself look better. However, I know our 15-year reputation in the business and community will withstand her fear-based deeds.

So, run your business as if you don't care what your competitors think about you. What they think makes no difference, because no matter what they think about you, you're going to do the best possible job you can for your clients. You're going to take ownership for any mistakes you make. You're going to educate and support your clients. You're going to earn every positive review and testimonial you get.

ADVISE YOUR CLIENTS WITHOUT EVER COMPROMISING YOUR INTEGRITY

Make sure you are always doing business at the highest level of integrity. Do not compromise your business. Do not compromise your clients. Live with the highest integrity so that you know that when a mistake happens, although it may cause frustration for people, we own it and we will solve it. Realtors should own that. Mortgage Brokers should own that. Every single individual involved in the real estate transaction needs to own that. These transactions are complex and mistakes happen, but they don't have to kill the deal if everyone owns their integrity and takes responsibility.

A very common mistake that I see is that the blame is put back on the client. I see it happen so many times, "Well, the client didn't get me this on time…" That's your fault. Don't blame the client for that. You're the service provider, not the client. Your client is paying your salary. That's your job. Take the integrity. Own your mistakes and move on. That's very important and I can't emphasize it enough.

LOVE TO HELP WITH AN OPEN HEART EVEN WHEN YOUR CLIENT'S HEART IS CLOSED

If your client is upset, just stay positive and encouraging. Let them know that you will do everything you can to get through this for them, and that you've got their back. Even if your client is not happy, you have to take this course. Not only may it help change that client's perspective, it will set your reputation firmly in the field.

If your client is angry with you, turn it around. Turn it around and create a great experience, and then go back and ask for a referral or testimonial. There is no better recommendation than when a client can share how you solved a frustration and pulled a deal together that might have fallen apart without your perseverance and commitment to the transaction. If that client can turn around and say, "That was a bumpy closing, but you got us through it," you've done your job, and you've done it well" Then you've done your job.

If you turn a client who has a closed heart into a client with an open heart, you now have an endless referral stream from that client. Guaranteed. You've created that relationship. You've basically become a hero in their eyes. Now, ask for that testimonial.

Send them a direct link within an email so that they can leave that review or testimonial in one quick, easy step. Once they provide that testimonial or review, respond to each and every one, thanking the client, or responding to any issues that they brought up. Engage with them and thank them for their review or testimonial.

RESCUE YOUR BUSINESS ASSIGNMENT

Write an email template that you can send to satisfied clients, including link to leave reviews or testimonials on a variety of platforms like Yelp, Google, your Facebook page or website.

What steps do you need to make to guarantee that you will get a positive review from every customer, for every transaction?

_____

_____

_____

_____

_____

Look at the testimonials of competitors or vendors in your field. What are they doing right? Where have they failed their clients?

_____

_____

_____

_____

_____

"Intelligence grows in a happy mind. When the public knows you know your industry, repeat referral business continues to flow smoothly. Education will never disappoint you."

Cynthia Benchick

Charles Rutenberg Realty, LLC

Chapter 10

Having a Successful Business Plan

We all know about the benefits of having a business plan; an idea of how you will run and grow your business. Most of the time these plans are written so that you can get financing for your new business, either through loans or grants/gifts. As useful as they can be, when we're being completely honest with ourselves, these plans usually end up on a shelf somewhere in our office and are rarely utilized as the powerful tool that they can be.

I refer to business plans a little differently than most. Since my business is referral based, and so should yours, instead, I have written a Referral Marketing Plan. I suggest you do the same, as it gives you some concrete steps and guidelines that you can use, every day, to grow your business. In writing our Referral Marketing Plan, I follow thirteen specific steps.

A lot of these steps you can go through fairly quickly, but some of them take more time. Bottom line, you need to have this marketing and business plan. It needs to be written down, and not just in your head. If you don't write it down, you can't be held accountable. So, take the time to do this; don't rush this part of your process. If you're an established business and already have a business plan, do this anyway. You'll come up with new ideas that will help you get to where you want to be as a business.

Let's dive in!

Step One: Mission Statement

This defines why you exist, and what the purpose of your business is. There are many resources available to help you draft this mission statement. Talk to colleagues, look at similar companies' mission statements, talk to friends, involve your staff. Whatever you decide for your mission statement, make sure it's written down and prominent in your business, as a reminder of what your purpose is, for everyone to see; you, your team, your vendors, your clients, etc.

Even if you are just a company of one person, you still need to write this down, so you understand your purpose and focus. Otherwise you will not be able to scale your business; you will limit your success and quite possibly fail if you don't have this type of direction. You will never achieve financial freedom without it.

Independence Title Mission Statement

To be the most efficient title company in the industry. We strive to empower our relationships with proven strategic alliances by offering competitive pricing and delivering a fast and efficient experience. This is accomplished by both anticipating the needs and exceeding the expectations of our clients.

Step Two: Know What You're Selling

Are you a Realtor? So, you help sell houses, right? If you're a mortgage lender, you sell loans. A title company? You sell title insurance. But, if you really believe that this is all you do, you are missing out on realizing incredible fulfilment, and success.

You see, I don't think you sell houses, or insurance, or loans; you sell feelings. You sell experiences. You sell dreams. You sell that feeling of walking into a new house. You sell the American Dream for first time homebuyers, or veterans. You sell the warm feeling of seeing kids playing in the backyard of the house, or the family gathering for Thanksgiving dinner in their new home. That's what you sell. So, the language that you use to define your products and services will help drive how you treat your clients, your team, your business, and your colleagues.

Step Three: Know Your Target Market

What is your target market? Is it a zip code? A subdivision? East of downtown? Beachfront condos? Successful Realtors, for example, tend to focus on a target market or places that they know they can nail. One of my target markets, for instance, are real estate investors that close 2 to 3 transactions per month and attend certain real estate clubs that I am a member of.

If you say your target market is "everywhere" or "everyone," you are going to fail; that's the antithesis of the word "target." Hone in on who and where you want to serve, and you can get as specific as you want, but only if you have enough business coming in. You may find that your target market becomes smaller and more specific as you start to understand your strengths and passions. But, bottom line, your target market is the person who believes in the same vision that you do. Only then will you get there, successfully and in a way where a positive experience is paramount.

Step Four: Know Your Competition

Who is your competition? How many deals are they doing a month? What are they doing? How are they doing it? How are they becoming so successful? Follow them on Facebook, look at their ads and find out all you can. There is enough business for everybody.

I look at what other companies are doing and try to replicate what I think will work by making it even better. You're not harming them, or saying anything bad about them, you're simply learning. Pay attention to any competitors and their social media content; what's getting great interaction and referrals? Create your own, then, and put your own personal spin on things.

Step Five: Matching Needs with Prospective Sources

You have to be able to match the needs of your clients with sources or other businesses that can help your client out. Whether it's an appraiser, a handyman, or other type of vendor. You want to be able to connect clients with people that you know, like and trust; you can then ensure that they will also have a great experience with that vendor.

By you referring people out, you become a central hub of information, and the go-to person when a client needs anything. You will create an automatic referral system, as those vendors will remember that you sent them clients who had great experiences. Remember, you are selling experiences, not a product or service. When a Realtor refers a client to me, I make sure that I make them look good; I make them shine. Network = Net Worth. If you have a good system of people around you, your business will shine and grow.

Step Six: Define Your Tactics

What are you doing? What steps are you taking to help someone achieve their dream? What tactics are you utilizing to create great success? Are you volunteering in the community? Are you spending time researching your market, legal aspects of real estate, community details like school districts? Are you discovering the details of your particular region or area? Are you seeking advice from people in your field, from other business owners? Are you learning as much as you can? If not, you should be!

Step Seven: Collaborate

Team up with some of your referral partners. Collaborate, socialize, create events together, put on first-time home buyer seminars and workshops. For example, when we design first-time home buyer seminars, we bring in a Realtor, a mortgage lender, and wow the client; we teach them how they can become a homeowner.

Step Eight: Create your Referral Marketing System

Put all of the above steps together to create the system that you will use to give and get referrals. If you don't develop a system, you will not succeed. You need to have that system written down, as well. For example, I look at key sources of business; where does your business come from? Who are your top ten clients, and how do you find ten more of those?

Meet with those top ten clients, brief them on what type of client you are looking for, and how they can help you connect and find those prospective clients. So, if I'm talking to a Realtor who is highly successful, I might ask them, "Who else do you know, in a different market, that is as successful as you are?" Your key sources of business become your referral sources.

Step Nine: Reward Your Key Sources

How do you thank and reward your key sources for helping generate referrals and resources? I'm not necessarily talking monetary rewards, it can just be a great experience. Maybe you meet them for coffee and ask how you can help them grow their business. In the past, I've offered opinions on helping design a logo, or coming up with a marketing plan, or educating a client on what I know about a new market they might want to be getting into.

Sometimes I find an interesting article that I think a client might like and send that along with a personal note. By rewarding them, you're recognizing them as one of your sources. Maybe it's recognizing them at an event that you put on. Maybe you take them to an event and introduce them as one of your referral sources. Maybe you can send them a new client source. Any way that you can thank and recognize them is a reward.

Step Ten: Create a Time Budget

I'm very regimented with my time, and I think most successful business owners and entrepreneurs are. Think about achievers like Warren Buffett other highly successful people; they all tend to have a strict Time Budget that they work from. In my business, I come in every day, and I start with the same task. Every. Single. Day. Start with the first task, then the next, then the next, and so on, throughout the day.

This will help you focus on everything else that we've talked about so far. What are your tasks that are going to generate referrals? You can assign yourself time budgets on a weekly basis, as well. For example, attend x number of networking meetings, and spend x number of hours weekly working on implementing a better referral marketing plan. Or, x number of hours every week sitting down with your referral partners and getting to know, like and trust them, so you can create better referral opportunities for each other.

You can revise your time budget by analyzing things; did you spend enough time marketing? Did you spend too much time answering emails? Did you spend enough time meeting with clients and referral resources? You can then re-adjust your Time Budget, accordingly. It's almost like conducting a cost-benefit analysis, but for your time.

Step Eleven: Use a Calendar

Every successful business venture tracks their appointments, deadlines, and timelines using a calendar program. Whether you're using Google calendar or Outlook, it doesn't matter. By organizing your appointments, you'll avoid embarrassing situations like double-booking a timeslot, forgetting an appointment or a deadline. Make sure that details include what, when, and where. You want to make sure nothing conflicts.

Step Twelve: Checks and Balances Statement

You need to know what money is coming in, and what money is going out. I use Excel for this; I track what I'm spending money on, and how that fits into the different tasks of my business and day. Tracking expenses for social media, marketing events, networking meetings, advertising and other aspects related to building my business helps me understand what's working for my dollar, and what's not.

Anything that you do in your business to create referral opportunities, you should establish a budget for, and then track your spending activity to make sure you're keeping to the budget. You can then analyze that budget and find out whether or not your money is being well spent for certain referral building activities. Maybe social media efforts bring in $100 for every $25 spent, but networking events are bringing in $500 for every $25. You can then make smart decisions on where to focus your efforts.

Step Thirteen: Create Sales and Referral Projections

This is something that I've been doing for many years, and still do it to this day. I have a spreadsheet to track this, to know how many deals I've done compared to the same month last year, the year before, and the year before. That way we can follow our sales and referral projections, so we know how many deals we need in order to be growing. Knowing how many prospects you need in order to close the deals that you need to grow your business is key to understanding where you need to spend your time and money.

The smartest way to figure this out is to work backwards. Let's say that you know that you need to close five deals a month to make a decent living. On average, it might take ten prospective interviews and meetings to get those five deals to close. So, you work toward achieving those prospects in order to get to the deals that you need. So, know your metrics; the only way to know these numbers is to understand your own business, this will take time, especially if you're new at this. For our business, for example, I know that I need to have 200 prospects in the pipeline at any given moment to get to the 100 deals a month that we would close from that.

We track these numbers in Excel, but there are a variety of software packages that can be used for this. Ask around with other colleagues and do the research to find out what will work best for you. Not one software solution is perfect, but you'll be able to find one that works for you. These programs can put value to each referral, to each average closing, and down to how much a prospect phone call or meeting is worth. You can almost project down to a few dollars how much you can expect to earn in any given week, month or year, with this type of tracking software.

Anyone who follows a successful business plan can be successful. These thirteen steps might seem overwhelming to you right now, especially if you're just getting started in this process, but don't panic. Take one at a time, maybe weekly. Meet with other people who have gone through similar planning and systems design, and put together what you think will work for you. It's likely that you'll have to change things up as you gain experience, and analyze what's working for you.

RESCUE YOUR BUSINESS ASSIGNMENT

Write down the Mission Statement of 3-5 successful competitors:

_____

_____

_____

_____

_____

_____

Draft 2-3 main points that you want to express within your Mission Statement:

_____

_____

_____

_____

_____

_____

_____

Write a first draft of your new Mission Statement, and share it with colleagues, friends and team members:

_____

_____

_____

_____

_____

_____

_____

_____

_____

_____

_____

_____

_____

_____

_____

_____

_____

_____

_____

"Be valuable to valuable people."

Mike Fallat

Owner of DreamStarters Publishing

Entrepreneur & Investor

Chapter 11

What to do when Running Out of Fuel

No matter who you are. No matter how long you've been doing what you're doing; if it's one week, or one decade. At some point, you're going to run out of fuel. Everyone does. Sometimes personal obligations seem overwhelming, sometimes the holidays can burn you out. Other times, maybe you're having a tough time closing new deals, or a critical team member leaves your organization. We are all susceptible to burnout.

When you run out of fuel, the most important thing to do is to recharge as quickly as possible in a healthy way. Maybe more importantly, don't wait until you're completely out of fuel to tackle this. Think of your cars; if you wait until you're completely out of fuel, you can cause damage to your car, and then you're also stranded. You have a fuel gauge in your car, and you should have a personal fuel gauge.

Monitor what it looks like for you when you are getting low on fuel. You want to re-fuel before it's too late, otherwise you will leave yourselves, your friends and your family stranded on the side of the road. Refuel before you hit rock bottom. Refuel before the market crashes again. Refuel before your deal dies. In any part of the business, if a deal is going south, you need to refuel before the deal is lost. Refuel, recharge and refocus and close your deal.

Now, this doesn't always work. Sometimes things happen where you're going to lose direction or lose that deal. But, if you run out of fuel, you're done. At that point, it's very hard to reset and refocus. Catch things, and recharge, before things get so low that you're at higher risk of losing out on current and potential business. When you're at that point, it will be almost impossible to bring your business to the next level, so it's important to catch things before you completely run out of energy and motivation.

As a successful business, you must always be launching into the next level. You need to make sure that you're not running out of fuel, you are recharging by meeting with people who empower you and motivate you. Surround yourself with people who will build you up and who will help you get to where you need to be. Having a great team in your business alone, can recharge your batteries. I don't know where I would be without my team. When I have a bad day, they can help lift me back up.

When I say, "don't run out of fuel," the word "fuel" can mean different things to different people. It can mean energy, money, momentum, or motivation. It can mean taking care of your body, mind and spirit by eating well, taking time to relax and recover, going to the gym, taking long walks, or spending quality time with your family. Personal and professional "fuel" often overlap. If things are draining on the business side, it can negatively affect your personal life, and vice versa.

Momentum requires fuel, and if you are moving in the right direction, your business and personal life will almost always automatically refuel things. The second you feel like your momentum is lost, you need to press the pause button and take a long hard look at that. Or, if you feel like your momentum is moving you in the wrong direction, you need to hit the brakes and redirect. So, for example, if you're maintaining statistics on sales, or marketing reach with YouTube views, and you see that they're moving down instead of moving up, you need to find out why. Don't let those numbers move down to zero or close to zero, because then the damage is done.

In addition to surrounding yourself with people who can help motivate you and keep you focused, other ways to recharge are taking vacations, or going for dinner with friends, colleagues and clients. For me, personally, I find that the best way to recharge my batteries and refocus is to surround myself with people who can help me do that. This goes back to something I spoke of earlier in this book, and that's my Board of Directors; my wife, friends, clients and colleagues who can give me advice, ideas and support.

This happens to the best of us. Sometimes if I'm feeling strained and overwhelmed, I'll go to my Board of Directors and say, "I'm having a tough day or week, and need some ideas and support." Asking for help is nothing to be ashamed of, and it can really get you out of difficult times. We'll talk about this further, later on in the book, when we discuss your support system, but for the purposes of this discussion, knowing you have the support of colleagues, family, friends, and clients, can help you stay on track and maintain fuel levels.

Sometimes I'll come home, and will be carrying on and on about the business, about the next steps, goals and tribulations. My wife will just look at me and say, "Can't you just turn it off for an hour?" I laugh, and say, "No." But, she's right. Even though that entrepreneurial trait is in me, where we never stop thinking about our business and how we can take things to the next level, you have to just STOP sometimes and be in the moment.

Our hard work and business is why we have the life we do; a nice home, the ability to travel, the ability to give back to our community. But, if I'm not paying attention to the quality of my family life, those batteries will burn out too, and I see too many people who sacrifice their family for their business, or vice versa. However, maximum success comes from taking care of all aspects of your life.

I've seen people reach rock-bottom. When I first started in this business, I had four partners, and unfortunately the crash of 2008/09 took all of us down. I saw my partners run out of fuel and give up on their dreams. I kept focusing on how I could get through the crash and grow beyond this temporary setback. I knew that I would eventually get through it and survive. All of my partners, instead, got out of the business and took their losses. They lost hope, and they lost focus.

That little bit of fuel that I kept in my tank is what saved me. It's what pushed me to the next level. I reached rock bottom, but I never gave up. In fact, a funny story is that at the worst of this time, in 2010, I attended a foreclosure workshop, and met my wife. She went there to learn how to buy foreclosed property, and I was there teaching others how to do the same. I wanted to hang out with other successful people, and through that met my wonderful wife Alana. We continue to work together, evolve, learn and love together.

RESCUE YOUR BUSINESS ASSIGNMENT

What are some effective ways you have to "recharge" your batteries?

_____

_____

_____

_____

How do you know you are getting low on fuel?

_____

_____

_____

_____

Have you built your Board of Directors, yet? If not, do so within the next 30 days!

_____

_____

_____

"Success is always next to hard work... There's no success without hard work. Take great care of your team and they will take great care of your business!"

David Gonzalez

Chapter 12

Building a Real Estate Dream Team

Whatever industry you're in, it's critical that you have people by your side. People to help you through the day to day struggles, and to help you reach your goals. Now, we're not talking about people who are doing exactly what you're doing, but people who complement what you're offering. So, in real estate, it might be partners and team members who are Realtors, mortgage brokers, title company managers, appraisers, attorneys, home inspectors, and so on.

When an investor calls me, for example, and needs an appraiser, I can spout off my favorite appraiser's name and phone number, instantly. The appraiser that I refer people to is on my dream team. You need to build your dream team and get to know them so that you can confidently refer clients to them. Then, you've built your referral machine and your dream team members will refer clients to you, as well.

If you have a team of professionals that you know you can count on, that you know will take care of your clients, you can sleep at night. These people are critical to your success and can make or break any organization. Having a dream team will help you solve any problem that you or your client may come across in any real estate transaction. But this goes beyond the initial transaction, too.

For example, maybe you just closed a deal for a family who has young children and a pet dog. They want to put in a fence around the swimming pool, or a fence around the yard, or both. If you have a dream team, they can call you and you can say, "Here's the company I recommend; they've done tons of great work around the area. Tell them I sent you." You can even anticipate this; if you're selling a house to a young couple, and the wife is six months pregnant, you can tell them, "Here's the name of a colleague who can make sure your new home and yard are safe for your baby that's on the way."

This dream team will help you get to the next level, and who will help you grow. If you have your dream team, they will constantly be talking about you and sending referrals your way. In turn, you'll constantly be referring clients to your dream team. This all goes along with your Referral Marketing Plan. These are your referral sources, in addition to your clients and prospects. Your dream team has the clients that you can service, as well, and vice versa. You can feed clients and deals to your dream team members.

To develop and nurture this dream team, meet with several vendors, and find out who will be the best fit. Then, meet with them regularly. Either individually, or as a group. Ask how you can help build their business and let them know how they can help you grow your business. Don't be shy about this; asking for referrals, so that everybody benefits, is the secret to building an endless referral stream for everybody on the team.

Some of my dream team members, who are vendors, affiliates and colleagues, have been working with me for the entirety of my career in real estate. These include my appraiser, lenders and Realtors. That's not to say I only refer to dream team members; sometimes my clients have different needs. But, networking as much as I do, I can refer my client to the best vendor, based on their needs and personality. I know who they're going to work best with.

I'm a big believer in the DISC program, which helps you understand people's' personalities and motivations. I became certified years ago, and it has really helped me grow my business, and match potential clients with dream team members, AND know which type of client would work best with me. I learned how to give presentations to cover all personality styles that we learn about in the DISC program, because I know that in an audience of 20, there may only be 2 or 3 who are like me, and motivated by the same things that I am.

DISC profiling can help you understand the personality and motivations of not only yourself and your clients, but also of your dream team members, employees and colleagues. You can then connect people who are going to work well together. If they are likely to work well together, they'll have a great experience, and come back to you for more business.

A short version of DISC personality styles are:

D - Dominance, no-nonsense, let's get this done, results oriented, challenge the status-quo

I - Influence, enthusiastic, collaboration, and love taking action

S - Steadiness, thrive on collaboration, and support those around them

C - Contentiousness, strives for accuracy, appreciate stability, like a challenge

Understanding, truly understanding our clientele, members of our dream team, and ourselves, can help us match people and referrals in a way that will help your business explode. If you know you're dealing with a predominant "C" personality, you know you need to come to the table with statistics and detailed information on their potential neighborhood, for example.

This all goes back to building a team and network of people you know, like and trust. Understanding how different personalities work well together, or clash, can help you do this and make sure that everyone has a great experience. I think any successful business can be more successful if you tailor to the needs and personality of the client.

Your dream team isn't static; it can change. I've had to leave dream team members because maybe they've done something to harm my client, or they didn't take ownership of a mistake. When that happens, that team member is no longer on my team. When I refer someone to a dream team member, it's like I'm referring myself; how you treat my client, is how you are treating me. And, I treat my dream team referrals the same way.

This whole business is reciprocal. So, if I'm sending referrals to dream team members, I hope that they will send referrals to me. If they are not trusting me enough to send me business, I'm going to meet with them and find out what I can do better. If they still do not send me business, then I need to find another dream team member. Again, it's "giver's gain," so I'm going to give referrals, and I'm going to help someone build their business, but it should be a two-way street.

RESCUE YOUR BUSINESS ASSIGNMENT

Identify potential dream team members in related or complementary fields, at least 5-7 to begin with:

_____

_____

_____

_____

_____

_____

Set up meeting dates with each of the above potential dream team members.

What can you offer your dream team members?

_____

_____

_____

_____

_____

_____

All things being equal, people will do business with, and refer business to, those people they know, like and trust."

Bob Burg

National Bestselling Author and Co-Author of

The Go-Giver and Go-Givers Sell More

Chapter 13

Leverage Social Media and Brand Recognition

In today's world, a business must be effectively tapping into social media in order to succeed. Social media is the first place people go; more than 75% of Americans report getting their news from sites like Facebook and Google. If someone is interested in doing business with you, the first thing they will do is look you up on Facebook and Google to see your ratings, reviews, and get an idea for the services you provide.

You could try to do this yourself, but I don't recommend it. You need to focus on your business and making sure you're building meaningful and plentiful relationships in the community to start generating endless referrals. Hire a specialist who can help you get your social media marketing up to speed, and get your brand out there immediately, and consistently.

Even though I work on our social media platforms, I spend more time working on my business rather than in my business. If you're bogged down posting on Facebook to try and attract potential customers, you're working **IN** your business, versus **ON** your business. In the beginning, you will need to work in your business more than you will need to once you are more established. Make sure you recognize that when it's time and strengthening your brand and social media presence is something that can easily be delegated to someone else; this will free you up with more time to work on your business.

Base your activities on social media on your Referral Marketing Plan, which we discussed previously. Make sure that all your marketing material matches, so that there are not inconsistencies between your media messages and determine what your brand strategy is. Different from just identifying your brand, brand strategy refers to HOW you will get your brand out there in the real estate community.

How can you be the Coca Cola of the local real estate industry? When people think about soda products, their mind often jumps to Coca Cola and Pepsi. How do you get in the front of peoples' minds when people think of real estate transactions? You have to think about how you can put yourself out there to become a "brand name."

A very common mistake that I see business owners make is that they jump into social media with no strong brand, or message, or their message is inconsistent with what they are trying to do as a business. Facebook is easy if you want to quickly promote your business; simply press the "boost" button and pay a few bucks. But, it's a waste of money if you don't have a following; no one will see your "boost."

Over and over I hear from people who are posting 2, 3, 4 times a day on their business Facebook page, and they are frustrated that their phone isn't ringing with potential customers lining up to do business with them. That's because they're doing it wrong. I have a team that helps me with social media and we find it is very helpful to feed new customers into our lead program.

The team tracks all of our social media and online ad activities; whether it's Facebook, Google, Instagram, or our website. The team tracks activity, helps with branding, building capture pages on our website, responding to emails and social media messages; there's a lot that goes into social media beyond just sharing a post to your page, and waiting for your phone to ring.

The basics start with a high-quality website, including testimonials (see the previous chapter on this topic), contact forms and follow-up. Share details on the local market, including houses on the market that are interesting and/or particularly attractive. Get some good content on there and update it often enough so that when people visit your website, they'll see that you're an active real estate professional.

In the beginning, spend a little bit of time on social media, but don't spend a ton of time until you have the money to invest in proper, paid promotions and social media activity. Most Realtor Boards give their Realtors a mobile app that you can brand; so make sure to utilize this as a tool for your clients. This is a terrific marketing tool that you can put into the hands of your clients, literally in seconds.

Every real estate client wants to know what the value of potential properties are, so through these apps and social media messaging, you can set your client up on notifications that will inform them of any and all real estate activity in their prospective neighborhood. This information is also interesting for people who have already purchased property, so they feel like they got a good deal on their real estate investment.

What this is always about, is engagement with your clients, before, during and after the real estate transaction. If your buyer constantly gets updated by you on activity in their neighborhood, when they are ready to move and want to list their house, they'll call you first because they know you know the neighborhood. Social media is about social engagement. When I post a video to YouTube, it's not so much about getting the new client, but keeping current clients engaged and interested. This leads right into endless referrals.

Generating leads from social media often involves a financial and time commitment but can be well worth it. Showing up on social media, consistently, and in a way that informs and most importantly engages, will keep you at the forefront of people's' minds when they are considering a real estate transaction. It's time consuming but posting 1-2 times daily on social media is important for that consistency.

With that said, social media might not generate new business for you however, until you are willing to spend a high dollar amount on your social media marketing efforts. I'm not talking $10 to "boost" an ad; that's not going to work. What I'm suggesting is that you spend thousands of dollars on management and staff to target, re-market, and generate leads into referral opportunities.

Know your strategy, know your marketing plan, and figure out how much you're going to invest into social media. Before you invest large sums of money though, make sure your presence is consistent, daily, helpful, informative, and engaging. But, once you invest those dollars, it doesn't mean you disappear from your social media efforts. For example, I spend between 3-5 hours a day, working on my business with social media efforts. These activities include targeted following, commenting on other posts, posting on our page, and other things that increase brand awareness, including producing YouTube videos.

During the time that I spend daily, I'm also looking at analytics and statistics. What's working, what's getting a response, and what's not? What's leading to referrals, and what's not? How are my videos doing? Are we engaging with current and potential clients, with vendors, with colleagues? Are we keeping our brand in the forefront? Are the keywords working? Do I need to update the website with new content? I look at this every day.

Content has to be high-quality. It's not enough to just upload a video. It has to be informative, with good sound, clear picture, professional graphics and music. Don't shortcut this; invest in production value, because people will judge you and your commitment to quality, based on the quality of your content.

With everything you do, include a link and a call to action. Invite people to comment or answer a question. Make it easy for the viewer to engage with you personally. If they comment, answer back. If you post a video, make sure there is something for them to do as a result of the video, for example, "Call me today for information on your neighborhood, and how you can maximize your sales price."

Posting a picture on Facebook with no content, engagement or real information is a waste of your time, and people will not be interested in visiting your page very often. Unless you offer quality, useful and free content, people will just scroll right past. Placing targeted ads, with quality photographs, and engaging ad text that brings people to your website to ask for more information, which then goes into an auto-responder system, can be exceptionally effective.

I think it's also important to have a strong personal social media presence as well. For example, if I'm at an industry event or convention and I connect with someone one a personal basis, very often we shortly after become Facebook or Instagram friends or each other's followers. So, you can develop both aspects, personal and professional.

Realtors need to be careful in building their own brand, versus building the brand of their brokerage firm or company. At some point, you will switch real estate firms, and if you've spent most of your time building up the brokerage firm, you'll have a hard time re-establishing your identity in the market. You might spend 3-5 years at one firm, get a good client following, but if you're not marketing yourself, when you switch firms, it will be like you've disappeared off the face of the earth.

I've read many books on this topic, and one person's work that I highly recommend is Grant Cardone, author of titles such as, Sell or be Sold, and If You're Not First, You're Last. Take a look at how he markets himself via social media, and model some of his activities. His presence is huge with over 6 million followers. His materials and philosophy can help guide you as you build your own following on social media.

But, until you get there, be strategic. I get calls from people who see my Closing Cost Calculator popping up on all sorts of "random" websites. They ask me, "How do you do that?!" I laugh and say, "Because I'm following you!" That's what targeting does. Follow other people and businesses and engage on their pages, so that they will see you; not just on a banner ad, like my Closing Cost Calculator, but just in everyday discussion and dialogue. This type of presence takes time and a lot of money, so if you're just getting started, stick with the basics until you have money to invest in this kind of visibility.

When we up our marketing game, we take our list of all of our clients, vendors, colleagues, and social media connections, and we upload them as audiences in all of these social media platforms. We then make sure that everywhere our clients move around on the internet, we'll be in front of them. We are top-of-mind with relevant, positive, and informative content. You have to make yourself easy to find; they need to be able to know as much about you as possible, and know what you know and how you can help them.

As you build your social marketing team, make sure that you are having them focus on their strengths. Someone who is great on Facebook or Instagram, may not be so knowledgeable about Google. These two platforms are totally different beasts when it comes to online marketing presence. Make sure your team members are masters at whatever platform you are focusing on.

Hire a Facebook/Instagram master, and a different Google master. We have a different team for ad design and ad copy; these are two totally different skill sets, so don't try to combine them. We have another team that drafts the emails that people receive once the ad has led them into our lead and marketing system. As you can see, this social media thing is not easy or cheap, but once you master how it's done for your business, you'll reap the rewards with an endless referral stream.

RESCUE YOUR BUSINESS ASSIGNMENT

Research the Facebook and Instagram pages of successful competitors, as well as their website and other online presence. What are you noticing about how they are getting clients into a referral and lead generator?

_____

_____

_____

Evaluate your own social media presence. What are your strengths?

_____

_____

_____

_____

What are your weaknesses?

_____

_____

_____

_____

Make a list of 5 initial steps that you need to take in order to define and improve your brand recognition:

1.

2.

3.

4.

5.

"When dealing with clients... What I've always said as a golf instructor and now real estate wholesaler is that you're only as good as your last lesson or your last deal. So always treat your referral rolodex like gold!"

Jim Van Dyke

JVD Properties | Real Estate Wholesaler

Chapter 14

How to Get Started

I speak at a lot of networking and industry events, and a very common question is what this chapter is about. "How do I get started?"

They're often frustrated because they've attended a "get rich quick" seminar, which turned into a $300 weekend seminar, which turned into a $5,000 mentorship program, which then turned into a $50,000 "President's Club," or something like that. But, the bottom line, is that they're still stuck, they're still not really doing anything. They've never flipped a house or closed a significant deal that even comes close to paying for these expensive programs.

Maybe you're asking me that same question by reading this book. And, my answer is simple:

It starts with you!

Unless you are truly passionate about being a success or making money in this field - good money - then you will never succeed. Just because your neighbor, or sister, is getting rich in this business doesn't mean you'll be able to get rich, just by osmosis. Life doesn't work that way. You need to be 100% passionate about what you do, and 100% committed to the process, including its ups and downs on your way to a seven-figure income.

Some people can jump in and start in real estate with a 100% commitment to the field. Others can only dabble or need to do it part-time at first. That's fine. Just as long as whatever you're working on, you are fully committed to the level that you are on, at that time. If it's just an afterthought, and only an "occasionally I'll pay attention to this side-business of mine," forget it. You'll get frustrated, you'll waste your time and money and you won't succeed. So, ideally you should jump in full time; but, even if you can't, you can still be absolutely committed to making a great living in real estate.

Your mastery of what you want to do, and your passion, will be what brings you success. If you see yourself as solving problems for clients, and creating positive experiences, versus always chasing down the next deal, you'll be a success in this field. People ask me, for example, "Why don't you flip houses?" I say back, "Well, I don't want to - I'm not passionate about that." Sure, I have the skills, the licensure and the experience flipping homes, but it's not my passion.

So, I guess what I'm trying to say is that you need to start at the beginning. What are you passionate about? In this field of real estate, there are a million way to make lots of money; but what are YOU passionate about. What gets you excited? What challenges you in the best of ways? What are you most interested in?

Secondly, you need to make sure you have some basic funds to get started in your chosen field. Don't start a business on your credit card, or by securing debt. Stop! That goes with anything that you purchase to get things started. You'll end up working to pay off that debt, and not have any money left over for yourself.

If this means working and saving to get the funds you need to get a decent and professional start in your chosen specialty, do that! Don't start your business in debt. Scrimp and save and pinch pennies until you have enough to get a good, solid start.

Stop buying programs. Stop buying courses. Instead, go to networking events. Go to your local real estate events. Meet people;

talk to people and learn what they're doing. Then, implement the strategies that you see working for others and implement the strategies that you've read in this book. In a way, this entire book is about getting started, and what to do after that!

Build your foundation. Implement each of the steps outlined in the chapters of this book. Build your blocks with the basics of what we've outlined so far and go from there. Take your time, and don't put your cart before the horse. Move forward when you're ready, but don't be afraid of putting yourself out there without everything "perfectly" set up. Take little steps to get where you want to be, and don't expect any success to come overnight. Sure, you might land a big deal that will pay you for half the year, but if you're looking for something sustainable, then you have to be involved and engaged for the long run.

As you have made your way through this book, and you're ready to implement things, pick one skill or task and then master it. Once you've done that, move to the next. As you build your Referral Marketing Plan, for example, go through each of the 13 steps and tasks within that, one at a time, master a step, then move on to the next.

Likewise, as you determine your specialty and niche, learn that and master it. Don't try to do it all. Become an absolute expert and know your specialty inside and out. You should see yourself as the go-to person about X or Y. Back that assertion and brand up with real skills, and real insights that you can offer people who will need your help. Are you going to help buyers, or sellers? Pick one - don't try to do both. What part of your Local City or County are you going to focus on? Don't try and cover the entire region. Find your specialty and stick to it. Be the go-to expert that real estate professionals and consumers will seek out.

Understand the needs and expectations of your potential clients. Then, work backwards from there. If you decide your specialty is going to be beachside properties, talk to buyers about what they're looking for. Talk to sellers about what their experience has been. Talk to experts who have insured, inspected, and done work on beachfront properties. Know the school districts, test scores, school ratings, and everything a family would need to know about the area for their kids, their pets, and their in laws.

Part of your success is going to be something that you, and only you can control. You must absolutely have 100% faith in yourself, and confidence in your abilities. That's not to say that there isn't a learning curve and that you're not going to make mistakes. You will. What I'm saying here is that you have to believe in yourself and feel it in your bones that you're going to succeed, no matter what. That's where your self-education and mastery of whatever your specialty or niche comes in. At first, you may not know what you're doing, but you need to keep learning, and learning, and never be satisfied with what you think you know. Learn some more. Become a true master of your real estate craft.

Put in the hard work. Go all in. When I first got started, I was making cold calls. I would call in the evening, when people were getting home from work, and let them know how they could consolidate their debts and refinance their homes. I didn't necessarily enjoy making those calls, but I was all in and I was making a living. I was helping them solve their problems, I was closing loan after loan after loan.

If you are willing to do the hard work, and make the tough phone calls, there's no way you can't make it work if you follow the simple steps that I've outlined in this book. You can make it work, for sure! Stay positive and tell people the positive. No one wants to hear the negative. Be the person who solves problem. There are very few masters of what they do; if you can set yourself apart, by becoming a true master and being the best at what you do, you will succeed.

Attach yourself to and learn from masters in the field. For example, there are very few lawyers who specialize in real estate law. Learn from him or her. There are dozens and dozens of Realtors who get their license, compared to a master Realtor, who understands the market, and their niche, inside and out. Get to know that person and learn from them. Help them with referrals, get to know them, and get them to know, like and trust you.

What sets you apart? What is it about you that makes you different? When I first met my wife and she was coaching me on my business, she asked me why I never used my firefighter experience in my marketing. I hadn't even thought of it, but that whole notion of making sure that when there's trouble, I'm running in to it instead of running away, is something that I can show and do for my clients. We are all in this together. We go in and come out together. That's the firefighter way. That's how I treat my clients.

No matter what you do, when you're getting started, but also after you're well established, it's critical that you do the absolute best job that you can. Every day. Treat all your clients as if YOU are the client. What would good service look like to you? If you screw up and it hurts your client, how would YOU want it fixed if you were the client? Keep your ethics 100%. How you would want to be treated by someone you had hired? Build a reputation for 100% honesty, taking 100% responsibility for any screw ups, and giving 100% to your clients, your staff and your business.

At the beginning of this chapter, I spoke about the importance of knowing what you want and what your passion is. If we take that even further, it's critical that you know what your client wants and needs; maybe before they even do. Do the research, ask the questions, then ask follow-up questions.

Start at the end and work backwards. What I mean by this to ask the questions of your client, so they know, really know, what they want. What type of features in the home? How big of a yard? Do they want a pool? Do they have kids? Pets? What are some non-negotiables? What school district do they want to be in? Do they want a corner lot? To they want to be close to shopping areas? Generate a list of questions that you can ask your client to help them get to their vision, and then ONLY show them properties, products or services that fit what they're looking for, or come as close as you can find.

Fear stops people from getting started in this business, and if you're just getting started, look at fear differently than you have previously. Where there is fear, there's opportunity. Where there is opportunity, there's reward. Where there is crisis, there's opportunity. As long as you do things ethically, you'll be fine. The fear factor is going to be there, no matter what. In fact, if you aren't nervous or fearful a little bit, you're not being honest with yourself. It's when you let fear stop you from taking the next step, attending and speaking at the networking event, or making cold calls that's bad.

That nervousness is something that you can tap into. Let's say you're a little nervous to speak in front of an audience. That's ok; it's natural. That nervousness is there because you want to do a good job, and you want to be seen as an expert. Harness that nervousness by preparing, learning and educating yourself to answer any question with confidence. Use the nervousness to make sure you know your topic inside and out. Use that to connect with your audience; they are rooting for you.

Don't rehearse a script and give the same speech at each event. Connect with individuals in the audience and use your natural nervousness to prepare for a variety of audience members. Deliver what they want; connect with their emotions, their problems, their dreams. One of the best speakers I've seen when it comes to connecting with his audience is Tony Robbins. If you haven't already done so, watch a presentation of his and you'll see what I mean.

Remember, you are here to sell experiences, to help people reach their dreams, and to be the absolute best you can be. Take things one step at a time and know that if you are being true to your clients, you will achieve great success in this business. One step at a time. But you can't do any of this without your own personal support system. So, don't go it alone in life. Read on to Chapter 15!

RESCUE YOUR BUSINESS ASSIGNMENT

What are your passions in the real estate industry? Why?

_____

_____

_____

What steps will you take to become a master in your field?

_____

_____

_____

Develop a list of questions that you can ask a prospective
client to get at what they are really looking for and needing:

_____

_____

_____

_____

_____

_____

*"Say What You Mean, and
Mean What You Say, and
Everything Will Be Ok"*
Alana Burrell

Chapter 15

Having a Support System (Family)

In 2010, when I met my wife, Alana, at the Florida Foreclosure Convention in Fort Lauderdale, was when I realized I needed someone on my team; someone who could help me grow and learn as an entrepreneur but more importantly, as a human being. I had been married before, but I never felt like I had someone on my team; someone who always had my back.

I knew that if I was going to build a successful life, I needed someone who shared my vision for business and personal success. There are certain places, real and figurative, that I knew I needed someone to help me get there. My wife is probably the best person I've ever met who helped me get to where I needed to go. She believed in me, and in my vision for success.

Many times, I meet people at networking and industry events, and as I get to talking with them, I ask them where their spouse or business partner is. If they shrug and say something like, "Well, they don't really believe in this…." or "They're just not interested in this," I know they're in trouble. They should probably get out of the business, because it's not going to work.

A successful business is not a 9-5 job. My business does not stop when I leave the office; it continues. Sometimes I think my business gets productive when I'm not at the office and working on my business verses in my business. When I'm at the office, I'm in the daily tasks that I need to do to maintain the business. When I go home I'm strategically planning the tasks that grow the business.

Every relationship has challenges; I know this, for sure. But, if you don't have someone who believes in you, who shares your passion for what you do, and who supports you when you have to be away, or work extra hours, you're in for a hard fall. Most businesses never truly stop, so that sometimes means attending evening, weekend, or early morning events. If your partner is a Debbie Downer, and just complains about what you're doing, and how you're doing it, you need someone else in your life who will support you.

My success in business is in large part due to my wife Alana; her believing in me, and in my vision for this business. We work together. In fact, she was a Business Coach when we met and her involvement in my business helped me grow the business in leaps and bounds. Anytime I have a major problem, I bring her in. She's like the "big guns;" she sits down, and helps us get through it together.

I'm lucky. I have a built-in support system that will help me grow the business. You need that too, and if it can't come from a partner, or spouse, or if you're single, you need to build a support network. Maybe this is found in your Board of Directors. Maybe it's your top clients, or best friends. Either way, you need to feel supported through your ups and downs, your triumphs as well as your frustrations.

Your support system should have many folds. My support system's first fold is my wife and my family. It also includes friends, business managers, team members, colleagues, associates, and more. Your support system is also there to help you acknowledge your successes and celebrate them. Life is more enjoyable that way.

Sometimes your support system helps you through interruptions in life; for example, many times, we've gotten bad news while my wife and I are on vacation. It's ok, we say to each other, and we work our way through the problem, instead of letting it ruin our vacation. We rise to the challenge, deal with it together, and enjoy the rest of our relaxation time together. That's just life.

Any truly successful business is not grown from inside the office, it's grown from the outside. With that said, it's important to have boundaries when you get home, and have certain times when your talk about business is done. But, if things are really difficult professionally, it's hard to totally disconnect when you get home. My wife is a master at reading me, and sometimes tells me when I'm under too much stress. I try to cover things up, emotionally, sometimes; but it usually fails once I'm in the same room with my her, and she can see through my facade. Thank goodness for having her in my support network.

A good support network will help you solve problems better. When you try to tackle something on your own, it's impossible for you to see every angle and come up with a solution that factors things in. Put your ego aside and ask for help whenever you need it.

The main message here is that you can't do this alone. Make sure you have surrounded yourself with people who will support you, who believe in you and your vision, and who are willing to take the work, and give the time needed in order to succeed. This support network can include your significant other, your Board of Directors, your team, your best clients, your colleagues and vendors. Surround yourself with people who are cheering you on.

The life of an entrepreneur is very difficult; full of struggles and tough days. There are mental and physical struggles. When the market crashed in 2008 and 2009, some of the people who I thought supported me, disappeared and I was alone. I was basically left to drown and figure it out myself. How was I going to survive? It was the scariest time of my life. I had just moved down to Florida a few years before and had burned through all of my money. I really didn't know what I was going to do.

Yes, other people can help you, and you really do need that support system. However, the reality is that you work for yourself. In some very real ways, you are alone. I went from working for someone, to working on my own and my lack of college education meant that I had a lot to learn about how to run a successful business, and the skills needed to proceed. If you have a setback in your business, it's scary. So, you need a team to fall back on, and figure out a better marketing strategy, or a better way of doing things.

As you read through this book and you are working on your business, your goal should also include how to scale your business. In other words, if you're starting out as a real estate agent, my goal for you would be to become a broker, because you're scaling things where you have brokers representing you, and the business is growing because of that support network. So, when you build your support network, it can and should also include your business associates and team members. As they succeed, you succeed, and vice versa.

How do you know you have the right support system? Basically, if you are getting through tough times, or making difficult decisions, without unnecessary drama, you have the right team behind you. There will always be challenges and hiccups, but if a team member is always negative, and they aren't supporting the organization's vision and mission, you need to let them go. Life is hard enough as it is. Business is tough. You need to surround yourself with people who lift you up, and not drag you down; in your business and personal life.

One of the best business decisions I ever made was finding and nurturing a source for referrals. This launched my business; meeting that one real estate broker at a networking event and building a relationship that turned into a referral opportunity that continues to this day. We have a wonderful relationship that is a give-give arrangement. At that time, I had lost everything, so I risked everything to take advantage of this amazing experience. I packed up a U-Haul and moved into this broker's office. We never looked back, and it's one of the best decisions I've ever made.

Without her support and belief in me, I'm not sure I would have the success that I have. She is like another mother to me; she knew that I had hit rock bottom, saw that I was energized and ready to go. She even offered me discounted office space, for the first year. These kinds of opportunities come to you when you open yourself up to a support team who will help you get to the next level and develop your business.

RESCUE YOUR BUSINESS ASSIGNMENT

Who are your greatest supporters, and why?

_____

_____

_____

_____

How has someone helped you through difficult times?

_____

_____

_____

_____

How have you helped someone through tough times?

_____

_____

_____

_____

"Remember when teachers yelled at you for day dreaming in class? Well guess what? Successful people day dream in vivid color! Creating your success in a day dream can create your reality. The most powerful tool we posses is our mind. Our beliefs are very powerful and learning to harness them can create health, wealth and success. Our MindTalk can determine if we are going to be successful or ordinary. What will you create today?"

Yvonne Haase

LMHC, CHT International Holistic Center

RESCUE YOUR BUSINESS FINAL ASSIGNMENT

---

10 QUESTIONS EVERY ENTREPRENEUR SHOULD ASK
(By Patrick Bet-David – Value Entertainment)
www.PatrickBetDavid.com

1. What is your vision? Who do you want to be in that vision?

_____

_____

_____

_____

2. Who is your ideal customer?

_____

_____

_____

_____

3. How big do you want to scale your business?

_____

_____

_____

_____

4. Do you know what formula drives numbers in your business?

_____

_____

_____

_____

5. What are your weaknesses?

_____

_____

_____

_____

6. Where is time being wasted?

_____

_____

_____

_____

7. Are you working in your business or on your business?

_____

_____

_____

_____

8. What are some possible blind spots that you're avoiding?

_____

_____

_____

_____

9. What are your conversion ratios?

_____

_____

_____

_____

10. Who are the next 3 leaders you're building?

_____

_____

_____

_____

"We never feel completely ready for life's big decisions; but in taking the leap, we push ourselves to the next level."
Patrick Bet-David

Patrick is a successful start-up entrepreneur, CEO of PHP Agency, Inc., emerging author and Creator of Valuetainment on YouTube. As a natural critical thinker, Patrick takes complex leadership, management and entrepreneurial ideas and converts them into simple life lessons for today and tomorrow's entrepreneurs.

Thank you, I hope that you've enjoyed reading **Rescue Your Business** as much as I enjoyed creating it. If you can only remember a few things from this book, please remember the following important items:

- Always treat your network like GOLD!
- Make sure you give back to your local community!
- Invest in a mentor to take you to the next level!
- Don't be afraid to share your knowledge!
- Always plan for that stormy day!
- Start saving today for your path to financial freedom!
- Always focus on setting yourself apart from your competition!
- Learn something new each day to become a master at what you do!
- Ask your clients and referral partners to provide you with feedback and testimonials!
- Create and continue to update your Referral Marketing Plan!
- When you are running low on fuel, stop and refill!
- Make sure to build a dream team to be able to refer them to your best clients!
- Always have a positive forward moving presence on social media!
- Don't wait to get started, it will never happen on its own!
- Make sure you appreciate your support system both personally and professionally!

Please join me at the local real estate meetings that I attend in South Florida several times each month. I love working in real estate and I really enjoy speaking about it, so please make sure to introduce yourself!

If you enjoyed reading **Rescue Your Business** and would like to share your positive feedback and thoughts, I would be happy to post your positive testimonials on my website or on Amazon.com!

I hope that you choose **Independence Title** for your next closing, you can take comfort in knowing we've got you covered! I hope that you have learned something useful from this book that will help you build a 7-Figure Referral Based Business too!

I wish you good luck and great success as an entrepreneur, home buyer or seller, real estate investor or real estate professional.

Finally, remember to watch out for potential problems at your next closing to protect yourself from any costly issues in your real estate transactions!

Kevin Tacher, Founder & CEO
Amazon.com Best-Selling Author
Independence Title, Inc.
4700 W Prospect Rd, Suite 115
Fort Lauderdale, FL 33309
Phone: 954-335-9305
Email: Kevin@TitleRate.com
Web: www.TitleRate.com

TitleRate.com is the leading source for title insurance rates, real estate mobile applications, and up to date real estate information and education.

KEVIN TACHER

54298765R00083

Made in the USA
Columbia, SC
30 March 2019